INTRODUCTION

Write from the Start! Writing Lessons helps students with the kind of writing they do every day. Each lesson looks at a different type of writing. Some are imaginative text types, such as narratives and poems. Others are factual text types, such as reports and explanations.

All lessons begin with a sample text, which serves as a lesson model or for students to use as a reference when applying a strategy to their own writing. It is important that the text and special features of the sample models are read and discussed with students. (Note: Many of the sample texts used throughout the book have been written by students, which will make them even more enjoyable for your students to read and analyze.)

After the sample model has been introduced, students can work through the activities that follow. These give them guidance and practice in writing a similar type of text. The first activities in each lesson ask students to focus on the context of the sample model and reflect on what they read and how it was written. Additional activities direct students to the grammar and punctuation used in the model and how these apply to the text. Lessons also include activities that help students with vocabulary meaning and spelling. Every lesson ends with a "Your Turn to Write" section, where students apply what they have learned. This can serve as a reflection or assessment tool for each lesson.

In addition to the space provided on the activity pages of this book, it is recommended that students have their own journals or writer's notebooks. These can be used for some of the writing activities at the end of most lessons, where students may wish to extend their writing. A journal or notebook is also a good place for students to add references (illustrations, advertisements, photographs, research information, etc.) that they collect for future writing.

If you plan to use all of the lessons in the book, it is best to work through the book from Lesson 1 to the end. This will allow students to build on skills from one lesson to the next. However, each lesson can be taught independently. You may even wish to focus on a group of lessons that meet specific needs or standards. In either case, the format of this book allows for flexibility.

MEETING STANDARDS

The activities in this book meet the following writing standards, which are used with permission from McREL. Reading standards are also met by the "What Did You Read?" and "How Is It Written?" sections of each lesson; however, those standards are not listed below.

Copyright 2006 McREL. Mid-continent Research for Education and Learning.
Address: 2250 S. Parker Road, Suite 500, Aurora, CO 80014
Telephone: 303-377-0990 Website: *www.mcrel.org/standards-benchmarks*

Standard 1.   Uses the general skills and strategies of the writing process

1. Prewriting: Uses prewriting strategies to plan written work (Pages 11, 17, 23, 29, 35, 41, 47, 53, 59, 65, 68, 69)
2. Drafting and Revising: Uses strategies to draft and revise written work (Pages 11, 17, 23, 29, 35, 41, 47, 53, 59, 65, 68, 69)
3. Editing and Publishing: Uses strategies to edit and publish written work (Pages 11, 17, 23, 29, 35, 41, 47, 53, 59, 65, 68, 69)
4. Evaluates own and others' writing (Pages 25, 43, 49, 55, 61)
6. Uses strategies to write for a variety of purposes (Pages 23, 24, 36, 42, 48, 52, 53, 60, 66)
7. Writes expository compositions (Pages 6, 7, 11)
8. Writes narrative accounts, such as poems and stories (Pages 12, 13, 18, 19, 30, 35)
10. Writes expressive compositions (Page 65)
12. Writes personal letters (Pages 54 and 59)

Standard 2.   Uses the stylistic and rhetorical aspects of writing

1. Uses descriptive language that clarifies and enhances ideas (Pages 10, 28, 34, 37, 45, 46)
2. Uses paragraph form in writing (Pages 29, 41, 65)
3. Uses a variety of sentence structures in writing (Page 9)

Standard 3.   Uses grammatical and mechanical conventions in written compositions

2. Uses pronouns in written compositions (Page 57)
3. Uses nouns in written compositions (Pages 15, 16, 26, 39)
4. Uses verbs in written compositions (Pages 27, 33, 51)
5. Uses adjectives in written compositions (Pages 21, 31, 63)
6. Uses adverbs in written compositions (Page 45)
7. Uses coordinating conjunctions in written compositions (Page 57)
9. Uses conventions of spelling in written compositions (Pages 8, 14, 20, 32, 38, 40, 44, 50, 56, 62)
10. Uses conventions of capitalization in written compositions (Pages 9, 15, 33, 39, 58, 64)
11. Uses conventions of punctuation in written compositions (Pages 9, 15, 21, 27, 33, 45, 64)

Standard 4.   Gathers and uses information for research purposes

2. Uses encyclopedias to gather information for research topics (Page 29)
8. Uses strategies to compile information into written reports or summaries (Pages 29, 47, 68, 69)

Editor
Mary S. Jones, M.A.

Cover Artist
Delia Rubio

Editor in Chief
Karen J. Goldfluss, M.S. Ed.

Illustrator
Jan D'Silva

Art Production Manager
Kevin Barnes

Imaging
Leonard P. Swierski

Publisher
Mary D. Smith, M.S. Ed.

Author
Jane Baker

The classroom teacher may reproduce copies of materials in this book for classroom use only. Reproduction of any part for an entire school or school system is strictly prohibited. No part of this publication may be transmitted, stored, or recorded in any form without written permission from the publisher.

Teacher Created Resources, Inc.
6421 Industry Way
Westminster, CA 92683
www.teachercreated.com

ISBN: 978-1-4206-8071-3

© 2008 Teacher Created Resources, Inc.
Made in U.S.A.

TABLE OF CONTENTS

Introduction 3

Meeting Standards 4

To the Student 5

Lesson 1: Writing a Recount 6

Lesson 2: Writing a Narrative 12

Lesson 3: Writing a Poem 18

Lesson 4: Writing an Information Report 24

Lesson 5: Writing a Description of a Person 30

Lesson 6: Writing an Opinion Speech 36

Lesson 7: Writing to Persuade: Advertisement 42

Lesson 8: Writing a Procedure 48

Lesson 9: Writing an Invitation and a Thank-You Letter 54

Lesson 10: Writing a Response to a Picture 60

Lesson 11: Writing for School Research Projects 66

Answer Key 70

TO THE STUDENT

Dear Student,

When you use this book, you will be practicing recognizing and writing many of the text types you learn at school. Most of the sample texts (writing) in this book have been written by students in third grade. Carefully read the sample text at the beginning of each lesson and check which special features of the writing are highlighted or shown by arrows. Then work through the questions and exercises.

Work through the lessons from 1 to 11 in order. By doing this, you will build on skills and understanding from one lesson to the next. By the end of the book, you will have a good understanding of third-grade language and writing skills.

Good luck, and have fun.

Jane Baker
Author

LESSON 1 — Writing a Recount

A **recount** is a piece of writing that tells us about something that happened in the order that it happened.

STRUCTURE

Setting — who, when, where

Sequenced events — what happened in the order that it happened

Conclusion — ending, your personal comment

LANGUAGE

Facts about people and places

Time words clarify the order of events

Interesting details

Verbs all in past tense

OUR HOUSE REMOVAL

My dad built a house on our farm. It wasn't our house. It was a house he built for a man in Bungendore.

When it was finished, two men came to help us get the house ready to be moved. They cut the house into two halves with saws. Then they went away to have their lunch.

My friends Craig and Scott came to look at our house cut in two before it was towed away. They came because my mom called Mrs. Smith and invited them. Craig and Scott were still there when the men came back late in the afternoon.

The men came back in two trucks. Both trucks were semi-trailers. The men brought two big 6-foot-tall jacks with them. One man, named Carl, switched on a little motor to make the jacks move up and down.

The house was about 30 feet long. Each half was about 10 feet wide. The jacks lifted each half up high, then the trucks backed under them. Carl switched the little motor on again and the jacks went down. When they stopped the two house halves were sitting on the backs of the semi-trailers.

After my dad and the men made all the ropes tight, the trucks took the house away. We watched it go up the hill and out the gate.

Now the house is in Bungendore, and the man and his family live in it. I think they are happy in that house my dad built.

Kevin (age 7)

#8071 Write from the Start! Writing Lessons © Teacher Created Resources, Inc.

LESSON 1: WRITING A RECOUNT

☀ WHAT DID YOU READ?

① Who built the house? _____

② Where was the house built? _____

③ Where is the house now? _____

④ A crane loaded the house onto the trucks. **True or false?** _____

⑤ Carl turned a handle to raise the jacks. **True or false?** _____

⑥ **Circle** the names of Kevin's friends.

   a. Scott   **b.** Carl   **c.** Craig

⑦ **Circle** the correct answer. The house WAS / WAS NOT moved in one piece.

⑧ Can you explain why the ropes had to be tight? _____
_____

☀ HOW IS IT WRITTEN?

① The introduction tells us right away what the recount is about. **True or false?** _____

② **Circle** the **wrong** answer. Kevin gives us the measurements of the house to . . .

   a. show us how big the house was

   b. show why two semi-trailers were needed

   c. show off

③ Kevin tells us details of how things happened to make his recount more

   I _ T _ _ EST _ NG.

④ **Write** one interesting detail you learned from this recount about the way houses are moved.
_____

⑤ **Circle** the right answer. The writer tells us what happened in . . .

   a. any order   **b.** the order it happened

⑥ **Circle** the right answer. In the conclusion the writer tells us . . .

   a. what happened to the house and what he thinks about it

   b. what happened to the house

LESSON 1: WRITING A RECOUNT

SPELLING AND MEANING

Word Box	half	calf	shelf	elf
	halves	calves	shelves	elves

When you are learning to spell check for **spelling patterns** (e.g., elf → elves), use the Look, Say, Cover, Write, and Check method.

- **Look** carefully at the word.
- **Say** the word out loud.
- **Cover** the word.
- **Write** the word on a piece of paper.
- **Check** your word against the printed word.

Do this again and again until you are sure of how to spell the word.

Practice spelling the words in the word box using this method.

① **Circle** the right word.

    a. Ali ate both halfs / halves of the apple.

    b. The elves / elfs stitched the shoemaker's boots overnight.

    c. The cow was very proud of her little red calve / calf.

    d. Those shelves / shelfs are dusty.

② **Label** each picture correctly with a word from the word box.

 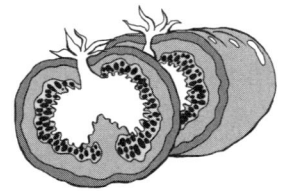  

a. _____ **b.** _____ **c.** _____ **d.** _____

③ **Insert** a word from the word box in the spaces.

    a. Rabbits ate _____ of my father's lettuce last night.

    b. Paint those metal _____ green to match the desks.

    c. Legends talk of mischievous little men called _____.

    d. Baby horses are called *foals* and baby cows are called _____.

    e. The two _____ of Earth are called *hemispheres*.

LESSON 1: WRITING A RECOUNT

GRAMMAR

All sentences contain at least one complete idea, and most sentences follow this pattern:

Someone/something → *doing* → *something*. We call this pattern **Subject** → **Verb** → **Object**.

Example: **My dad** (subject)   **built** (verb)   **a house** (object).

① **Circle** the subject, **underline** the verb (action word), and **draw a box** around the object.

   a. Neil Armstrong walked on the moon.
   b. Snakes eat small birds.
   c. Storm clouds fill the sky.
   d. Mr. Patel drives a moving truck.

② Are these complete sentences? Write **yes** or **no**.

   a. In the well. _____
   b. Lightning struck the old tree. _____
   c. The cyclone destroyed the old barn. _____
   d. Over the mountain range. _____

③ **Complete** these five sentences by **matching** the objects to their subjects and verbs. There is more than one right answer.

a.	Five children played
b.	All our class plays
c.	Mrs. Mercado packed
d.	A moving truck moved
e.	The garden tools are

in that shed.
her good china.
marbles.
soccer.
our furniture.

PUNCTUATION

All sentences start with a **capital letter**. Sentences that **tell** us something end with a **period**.

Example: Trucks, buses, and cars are all forms of transport.

Sentences that ask something end with a **question mark (?)**.

Example: Is a ship a form of transportation?

① **Insert** a **period** or a **question mark** at the end of these sentences.

   a. There are many different types of trucks
   b. Does Mr. Silvero drive a bus
   c. House-moving can be very exciting

② Help Josie punctuate her story. **Insert** all the **capital letters**, **periods**, and **question marks** that she has left out of the story below.

in the countryside there are no traffic jams to worry drivers. instead, drivers have to worry about dust. why is this so big trucks leave great clouds of dust in the air, and this makes it hard for drivers behind them to see where they are going

LESSON 1: WRITING A RECOUNT

FUN WITH WORDS

① What am I?

  a. I have four legs, hooves, and a long, swishing tail. The sound I make rhymes with ZOO. I am a _____.

  b. We are two flat, rectangular pieces of wood set in a frame. We are friends with glasses, vases, and books. We are _____.

  c. We wear little pointed caps and we like helping shoemakers at midnight. We are _____.

  d. I'm what you get when you cut an apple into two equal parts. I am a _____.

② Do you know who I am?

  My legs are long and gangling. My tail is as long as my legs. My bed is a furry pocket that moves.

  I am a baby K __ __ G __ __ __ O. I am called a J __ __ Y.

③ These are all words that have to do with house-moving. Can you **unscramble** them?

  a. URNTIFURE _____   **b.** OXBES _____

  c. RUCKT _____   **d.** CKPA _____

  e. MOVALRE _____   **f.** WRPA _____

④ Part of learning English is learning to speak clearly. **Practice** this tongue-twister.

  Jack wanted to jack up the Jaguar with a big jack, but John wanted the big jack to jack up the Jeep. Jack had to jack up the Jaguar with just a little jack, so John was joyful and Jack was not, when they were jacking up John's Jeep and Jack's Jaguar.

  a. Time yourself. 1st try _____ seconds 2nd try _____ seconds 3rd try _____ seconds

  b. How quickly can you say it without getting mixed up? _____ seconds

YOUR TURN TO WRITE

> TIP FOR TOP WRITERS!
> When you write a recount, make a plan before you start. First number the events in your recount according to the order in which they happened. Then write your recount in this order, starting with the first event and ending with the last.

LESSON 1: WRITING A RECOUNT

YOUR TURN TO WRITE (cont.)

① Help Ben and Ivan recount their house-moving experience by **numbering** what they did in the correct order.

a. wave goodbye ___	b. pack boxes ___
c. load furniture ___	d. load boxes ___
e. wake early ___	f. drive away ___

② **Draft** your own recount of something exciting that has happened in your family by following the instructions below.

    a. List all the events of your recount in the right order.

_____
_____
_____
_____
_____
_____
_____

    b. Write a **setting** to start your recount.

_____
_____
_____
_____
_____

    c. Write a **personal comment** to end your recount.

_____
_____
_____
_____
_____

③ **Write** your final **recount** on a separate piece of paper using the setting, list of events, and personal comment you have written above as your guide. Be sure to check for spelling, punctuation, and capitalization.

LESSON 2 — Writing a Narrative

A **narrative** tells a story. It can be a real story or an imaginary story. Which type do you think the story below is?

STRUCTURE | **LANGUAGE**

BEACH FIND

Fifteen years ago I was fishing in a boat with my dog Gruff. We were anchored off the beach when a big, black fin cruised up beside us. It was a huge dolphin.

She *whistled and clicked* and told us, "King Triton wants to see you." Then she swallowed us.

We had a rough trip down to the ocean floor where we were *spat* out on the sand. There in front of us we saw the mighty King Triton. He barked some orders to a starfish who sped away.

Half an hour later the starfish returned. Behind him *trailed* other poor people and their dogs. They all had worried faces like ours. "The king is about to make an announcement," *hissed* the starfish.

The king *glared* at us.

"Landcrabs," he began. *"You will build me a house for every creature in my world, even the smallest of them."*

We are still building those houses, even after fifteen years. All we eat is seaweed and plankton.

Before I put this in a bottle I must warn you: Never, ever trust a dolphin.

Please help us.

Gruff and Peter Small

Stephanie (age 8)

- *Setting* — who, what, where, when
- *Problem* — sequence of events that make up the story
- *Resolution* — story ends
- *Comment* — personal comment about what happened in the story
- *Interesting verbs*
- *Past tense* — all verbs in past tense
- *Direct speech* — exact words the character says

LESSON 2: WRITING A NARRATIVE

WHAT DID YOU READ?

① The title is "Beach Find." What was found on the beach? _____

② **Circle** the correct answer. This story is about . . .

   a. a dog   **b**. a boy and a dolphin   **c**. a request for rescue

③ How did the dolphin carry Gruff and Peter to the sea floor? _____

④ Who was King Triton's servant? _____

⑤ How do you think the other people and their dogs ended up in Triton's kingdom?
_____

⑥ How long have Peter and Gruff been building houses for Triton? _____

⑦ **a**. Did Triton feed his people? _____

   b. How do you know? _____

⑧ **Circle** the **wrong** answer.

   Peter put his message in a bottle . . .

   a. to keep it dry   **b**. so it would float to shore   **c**. to use an unusual container

HOW IS IT WRITTEN?

① **Circle** the correct answer. The problem of the story is . . .

   a. going fishing   **b**. the years of imprisonment   **c**. the chance of rescue

② **Circle** the correct answer. Where the characters were and what they were doing at the time of capture is found in the . . .

   a. setting   **b**. problem   **c**. resolution

③ Stephanie has chosen her words carefully. She uses just one word to tell us that the prisoners walked slowly and unhappily. What is it?
T _ _ _ _ ED

④ Direct speech (someone's own words) is a good way of letting someone in the story show what sort of a person they are.
Triton calls his prisoners _ _ _ _ _ _ _ _. This word tells us he thinks he is very important and that he DOES / DOES NOT like people. (Circle one.)

⑤ **Find** one example of direct speech from the text and write it here. _____
_____

LESSON 2: WRITING A NARRATIVE

SPELLING AND MEANING

Word Box	anchor	dolphin	whistle	mighty
	cruise	creature	trail	ocean
	rough	seaweed	click	plankton

Practice the Look, Say, Cover, Write, and Check way to spell with the above words (see page 8).

① **Draw** an ocean picture in the box below. Include as many of the ocean words in the word box as you can and write their names on them. Add any other ocean words that you know to make it interesting.

② **Match** the words in column **A** with their meanings in column **B**.

	A
a.	plankton
b.	click
c.	creature
d.	oceans

B
any living animal or person
very tiny sea creatures
bodies of saltwater covering ¾ of Earth
sharp, snapping sound

③ a. –**ough** is a common spelling for the sound –**uff**. Can you **complete** the table?

–ough word	Meaning
rough	not smooth
	strong
	sufficient

b. –**ui** is a common spelling for the sound –**oo**. Can you **complete** the table?

–ui word	Meaning
cruise	sail slowly
	apples and oranges are types of this
	when you bump your skin you can get this

LESSON 2: WRITING A NARRATIVE

✹ GRAMMAR

Writing is like building. It has tools and special ways to use them. Words are our tools. There are many kinds of words and each kind has a special use.

Some words are **naming** words. We call them **nouns**. Nouns name people, places, things, and ideas.

Example: When the **ship** sank, the **passengers** took to the **lifeboats**.

① **Circle** the words that are nouns.

cupboard	Monday	pretty	horse	America
happy	field	church	walked	shop
ship	illness	round	climb	George

② **Underline** all the nouns in these sentences.
   a. Charlie goes to the beach for the sun, sand, and surf.
   b. Flags on the beach show where it is safe to swim.
   c. Seashells are the homes of tiny mollusks.
   d. Starfish have bright red points along their five arms.
   e. The tide rises and falls according to the moon.

③ **Label** all the nouns in the picture below, including the parts of the dolphin (e.g., fin).

✹ PUNCTUATION

This writer was in a hurry and forgot to put in **capital letters** and **periods**. Can you help? Remember: each sentence starts with a capital, contains at least one idea, and ends with a period.

when winter is over, everyone is happy people wear sandals and sun hats children go swimming adults begin to garden again small plants grow tall and seeds turn into plants even birds are happy and busy building nests

LESSON 2: WRITING A NARRATIVE

FUN WITH WORDS

① Sea puzzles:

  a. What has eight arms and swims? An O __ T __ P __ S.

  b. A dog's baby is a pup—so is a SH __ __ K'S and a S __ __ L'S.

  c. A whale's baby, like a cow's, is called a C __ __ __.

  d. A horse that has no legs and cannot lie down is a S __ __ HORSE.

  e. A fish you might think is a fighter is a S __ __ __ DFISH.

  f. Did it fall from the sky into the sea? The S __ __ RFISH.

② Fill in the missing letters and then write all of the first letters in order (in letter **f.** below) to find the mystery word.

  a. A container: __ __ X

  b. A motor: __ NG __ N __

  c. Very upset: __ N __ __ Y

  d. A bear's baby: __ __ B

  e. Not solid: __ O __ LOW

  f. The mystery word is __ __ __ __ __. (Clue: I am washed by the surf.)

③ a. The Great Barrier Reef puzzle: I grow like a plant and I look like a plant, but I am really a tiny animal that likes to live in a group with others like me. I am C __ R __ L.

  b. The Great Southern Ocean puzzle: I am the biggest animal in the world and the largest in my family. I only eat plankton because I have no teeth. I am the BLUE W __ __ LE.

④ Write the nouns from the box beside the parts of the ship they name.

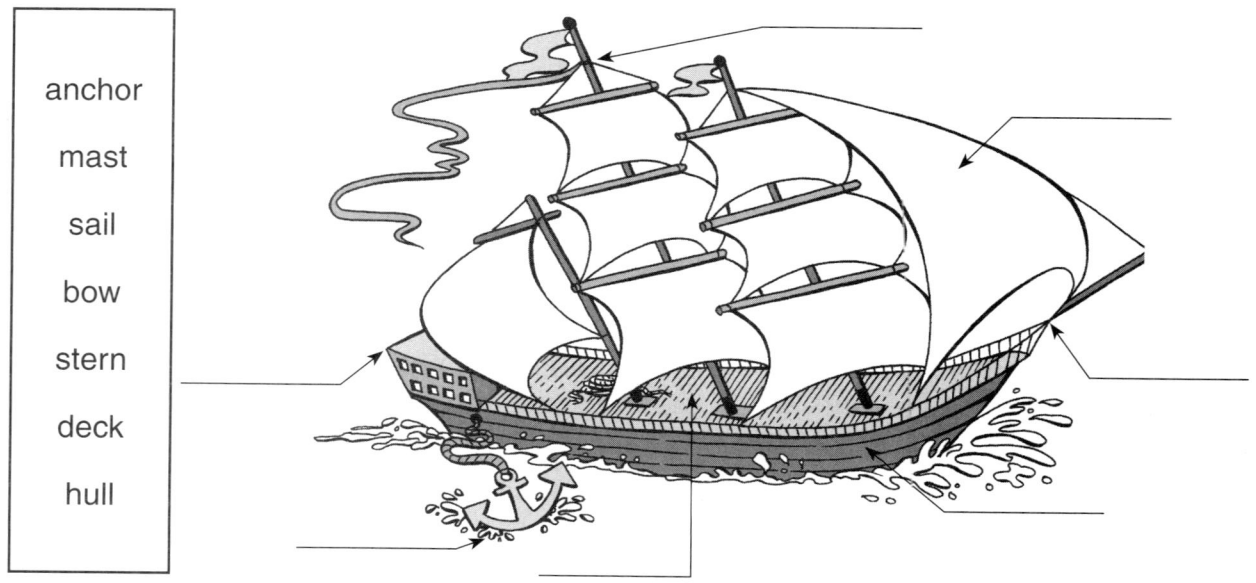

anchor
mast
sail
bow
stern
deck
hull

LESSON 2: WRITING A NARRATIVE

 **YOUR TURN TO WRITE**

> TIP FOR TOP WRITERS!
> When you write a narrative, try to include interesting information about people and places. This helps the reader feel like he or she is part of the story.

Imagine going fishing and having an adventure at the same time. **Outline** a story about it in the space below. Then **write** your final draft on a separate sheet of paper.

These are some ideas that might help you. You do not have to use them if you have a story of your own in mind.

- You fell out of the boat and had to be rescued.
- You caught a big silver fish.
- You saw a mermaid on the rocks.
- You met King Triton.
- The tide went out and you had to walk back over mudflats.

Title _____

Setting _____

Problem _____

_____
_____
_____
_____
_____
_____
_____
_____
_____
_____

Resolution _____

_____
_____

LESSON 3 — Writing a Poem

A **poem** is a word picture so clear that people can see and hear what the poet is writing about.

STRUCTURE — **LANGUAGE**

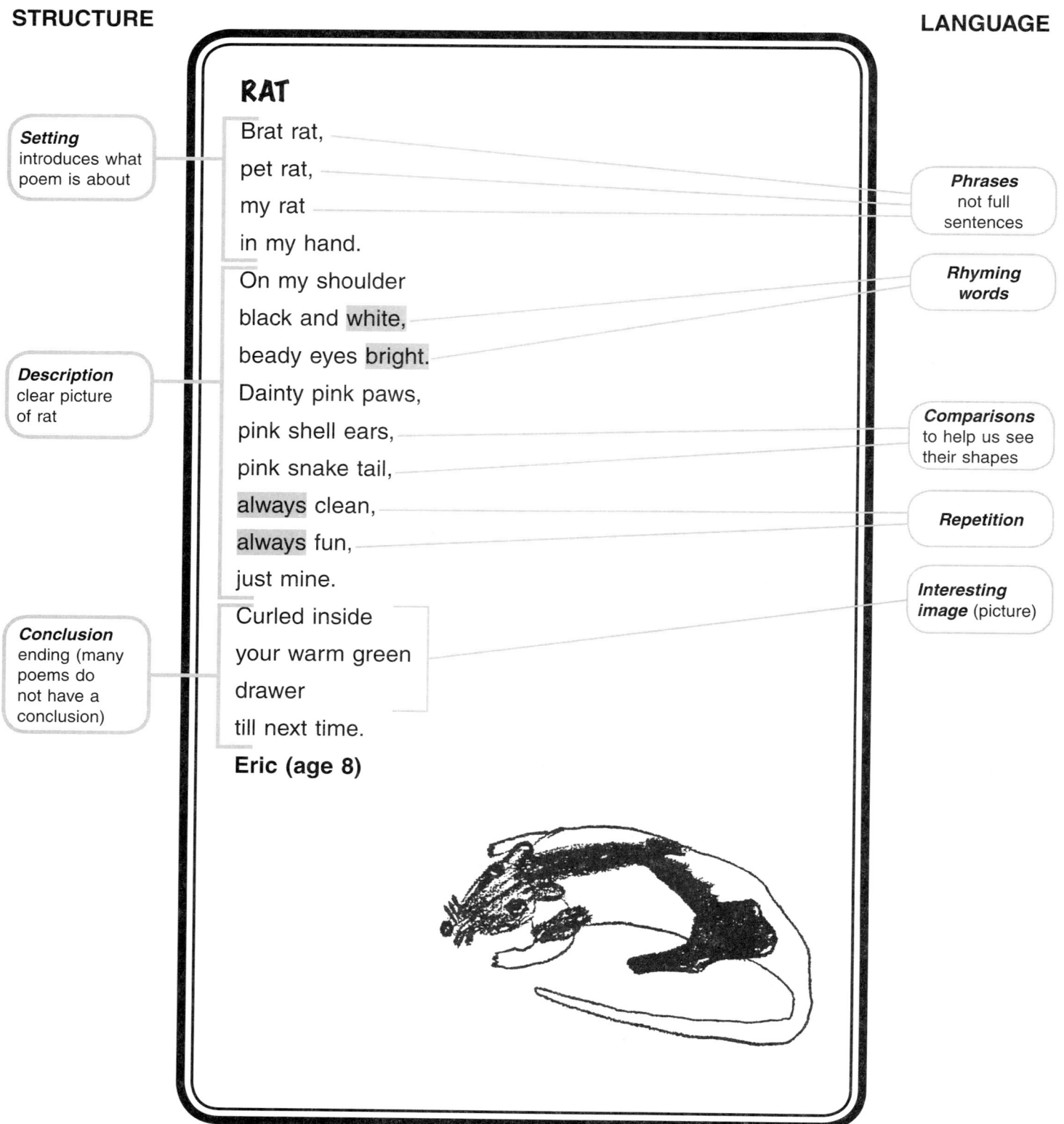

RAT

Brat rat,
pet rat,
my rat
in my hand.
On my shoulder
black and white,
beady eyes bright.
Dainty pink paws,
pink shell ears,
pink snake tail,
always clean,
always fun,
just mine.
Curled inside
your warm green
drawer
till next time.

Eric (age 8)

Structure labels:
- **Setting** introduces what poem is about
- **Description** clear picture of rat
- **Conclusion** ending (many poems do not have a conclusion)

Language labels:
- **Phrases** not full sentences
- **Rhyming words**
- **Comparisons** to help us see their shapes
- **Repetition**
- **Interesting image** (picture)

LESSON 3: WRITING A POEM

🌀 WHAT DID YOU READ?

① **Circle** the correct answer. This poem is about . . .

   a. a brat   **b.** a boy   **c.** a rat

② The rat lives in a cage. **True or false?** _____

③ How do we know this rat is not afraid of people? _____
_____

④ **Circle** the correct answer. *Brat rat / pet rat* tells us that this rat is . . .

   a. always good   **b.** sometimes good   **c.** always bad

⑤ **Underline** the correct word. The rat has ROUND / OVAL eyes.

⑥ The rat sleeps lying straight. **True or false?** _____

⑦ Does the rat's tail have fur on it? _____

⑧ **Circle** the correct answer. Eric's picture of his rat is . . .

   a. a gentle picture   **b.** an angry picture   **c.** a cruel picture

🌀 HOW IS IT WRITTEN?

① Eric's poem is not written in full sentences. It is written in phrases. **Write** the phrases Eric used instead of saying *My pet rat, that is sometimes a brat, is in my hand.*
_____
_____

② *Hand/band* is an example of **rhyme**. Find two lines in the poem where the end words rhyme.
_____
_____

③ To tell us his rat has round ears, the writer describes them as being like _____.

④ To tell us the rat's tail is long, thin, and round, the writer describes it as being like a
_____.

⑤ **Circle** the correct answer. *Dainty* tells us the rat's paws are . . .

   a. small and fine   **b.** small and sharp   **c.** small and ugly

⑥ **Circle** three correct answers. What feeling do we get from these lines?

   Curled inside

   your warm green

   drawer

   a. safety   **b.** comfort   **c.** fear   **d.** unhappiness   **e.** contentment

©Teacher Created Resources, Inc.

LESSON 3: WRITING A POEM

SPELLING AND MEANING

Word Box

beady	dainty	bright
lead	paint	tight
beach	saint	sight
reach	faint	light

Each column in the word box follows a special **spelling pattern**. When you learn these words, make sure you learn the pattern, too. Patterns make learning new words easy.

① Complete these sentences with words from the word box.

  a. Don't forget to use sunscreen when you're playing _____.
  b. If you look at the sun you will damage your _____.
  c. Artists _____ in oils and water colors.
  d. The _____ of the moon fades as time passes.
  e. Mrs. Najif made the _____ lace on that wedding dress.

② Choose a word from the word box to label each of these pictures.

  a. _____   b. _____   c. _____

③ Can you make –ea words to complete these sentences?

  a. Would you TEA __ __ me to play cards?
  b. Could you REA __ __ the jar on that shelf, please?
  c. Where is the dog's __ EASH? I want to take him for a walk.

  ⁀. Find words from the word box to match these meanings:

   ⁀ility to see _____
       ⁀rk _____
          ⁀f loose _____

            sentence: The three words in 4a, above, share the __ __ __ __

20

LESSON 3: WRITING A POEM

☀ GRAMMAR

Adjectives are words that **describe** nouns. They tell us about color, size, shape, age, feeling, taste, touch, and sound. In fact, they tell us all those things we know about through our senses.

Example: A rat needs a **warm**, **safe** house with plenty of **fresh** water.

① Underline all the adjectives in these sentences.
   a. Seals have sleek, smooth, brown fur and black eyes.
   b. Emus have long, bare necks, strong legs, and tiny, useless wings.
   c. The house was old and shabby with crooked walls and a chimney.
   d. Sweet-smelling sawdust makes a comfortable home for pet mice.
   e. In the empty park, a sad boy searched for his lost dog.

Adjectives don't always come before a noun. Sometimes they stand alone after words like *is*, *are*, *was*, and *were*.

Example: The new pups are **black** and **white**.

② Underline all the adjectives in these sentences.
   a. New foals and calves are always clumsy.
   b. Inoki was always happy watching tropical fish in the glass tank.
   c. Kate, Mira, and Selena were all in the same class and never lonely.
   d. Rough play can frighten a dog into becoming a bad-tempered dog.
   e. Green tree snakes make gentle pets.

Sometimes we can make adjectives out of nouns. A common ending for an adjective is *–y*.

Example: **bead → beady**

③ Can you **make adjectives** out of these nouns? Be careful of the last three.

Noun	Adjective	Noun	Adjective
a. leaf		b. sand	
c. dirt		d. anger	
e. hunger		f. friend	

☀ PUNCTUATION

We use a **comma (,)** to separate a group of adjectives from each other.

Example: The common garden mouse is a **quick, small, gray** thief of food scraps.

Insert all the missing commas in the following sentences.
   a. Seal pups are fat round roly-poly balls of soft fur.
   b. Magpies build big strong nests high up off the ground.
   c. Crimson rosellas flash scarlet blue and green in flight.
   d. Keeping pets is an interesting enjoyable and responsible hobby.

LESSON 3: WRITING A POEM

FUN WITH WORDS

| ~~eagle~~ | rat | mouse | frog | snake | guinea pig | magpie | goldfish | wombat |
| dog | python | lizard | cat | whale | penguin | canary | parrot | bear |

① Can you **sort** the words in the box into the right columns? (The first is done for you.)

Scales	Fur	Feathers	Skin
		eagle	

② Most animal homes have a name (e.g., a bird has a nest). Can you **match** these animals to their homes?

a. pig
b. horse
c. rabbit
d. fox
e. chicken

stable
burrow
coop
sty
den

③ There are special names for people who work with animals, too. Use a dictionary to help you.

   a. I study animal behavior: Z __ __ L __ G __ ST

   b. I look after bees: AP __ __ RIST

   c. I look after cattle and sheep: ST __ __ KM __ N

   d. I look after sick animals: V __ __ ER __ NARI __ N

LESSON 3: WRITING A POEM

FUN WITH WORDS (cont.)

④ Following the pattern **ring is to finger as sock is to shoe**, complete the following associations. You have been given a clue to each of the answers.

   a. Scales are to fish as F __ __ is to cats.

   b. Wool is to sheep as F __ __ __ __ __ __ __ are to birds.

   c. Web is to spider as B __ __ __ __ __ is to rabbit.

   d. Beak is to hen as B __ __ __ is to duck.

   e. Sky is to eagle as O __ __ __ __ is to whale.

   f. Claws are to birds as H __ __ __ __ __ are to horses.

YOUR TURN TO WRITE

> **TIP FOR TOP WRITERS!**
> The best poetry sounds like singing. Good poets . . .
> - often use **short phrases** instead of full sentences
> - choose their **adjectives** carefully
> - use **rhyming** words
> - **repeat** words and phrases

① Eric wrote this about his rat: **pink shell ears, pink snake tail,**

Think about the shapes and colors of these animals and to what you might compare them. Then **write two lines** that let us see your animal clearly.

Pig   Dog

_____   _____

_____   _____

② Another way of writing a poem about an animal is to **list** everything you know about it in single words. Read the two examples and then write two of your own about any animal.

Soft	Hissing	_____	_____
silent	spitting	_____	_____
green-eyed	yowling	_____	_____
curled	clawing	_____	_____
content	scratching	_____	_____
CAT	CAT	_____	_____

③ Now that you have practiced writing poetry, try writing a poem all by yourself about any animal you like. Use a separate piece of paper.

LESSON 4: Writing an Information Report

An **information report** is a piece of writing that informs the reader. Reports contain only **facts**. They do not include opinions (what the writer thinks).

STRUCTURE

Introduction usually includes a definition

Organized information new paragraph for each new development

LANGUAGE

All fact, no opinion

Technical words

Present tense all verbs in present tense

LIFE CYCLE OF THE BUTTERFLY

Butterflies are caterpillars when they are born. All caterpillars become butterflies unless something happens to them first.

1. Their lives progress through different stages. First, the butterfly eggs lie on the leaves of plants where their mother laid them. Next, the eggs hatch and the little caterpillars climb out.

2. The caterpillar eats and eats. It eats leaves and grows fat.

3. Soon the caterpillar builds a large outer shell around itself. It stays inside that chrysalis for more than two weeks.

4. Finally, the chrysalis splits and the new, beautiful butterfly emerges. It sits in the sun until its wings are dry and strong. Then it flies away to sit on flowers and collect pollen. As it flies from flower to flower, it mixes different pollens and helps more flowers grow.

Anthea (age 8)

LESSON 4: WRITING AN INFORMATION REPORT

WHAT DID YOU READ?

① **Circle** the correct answer. The life cycle of a butterfly starts when it is . . .

   a. a caterpillar

   b. an egg

   c. a butterfly

② What hatches out of the egg? _____

③ What does the caterpillar eat? _____

④ When it has grown big and fat, what does the caterpillar do?
_____

⑤ **Circle** the correct answer. The chrysalis is used as . . .

   a. a shelter

   b. a box for food

   c. to make silk

⑥ The new butterfly waits for its wings to __ __ __ before it flies.

⑦ Why does the butterfly visit flowers? _____

HOW IS IT WRITTEN?

① A report tells us facts about something. **Write** two facts that you find in the first paragraph.
_____
_____

② A report uses technical words. **Find** the technical words in this report that mean . . .

   a. what an egg does to produce new life: __ __ __ __ __

   b. the fertile yellow dust at the center of a flower: __ __ __ __ __ __

③ **Circle** the correct answer.
Sometimes a report is followed by a diagram. Anthea's diagram shows . . .

   a. a chrysalis

   b. the life cycle of a butterfly

④ **Circle** the correct answer. The diagram gives the same information as the report . . .

   a. to fill up space

   b. to add interest to the report

   c. to illustrate the connections between the facts in the report

LESSON 4: WRITING AN INFORMATION REPORT

SPELLING AND MEANING

Word Box	butterfly	different	hatch	leaves
	caterpillar	stage	collect	beautiful
	pollen	build	chrysalis	emerge

① **Insert** a word from the word box in each of the spaces below.

  a. Bees, like butterflies, gather _____ from flowers.

  b. The _____ of some trees turn scarlet and gold in autumn.

  c. John was as snug in his bed as a caterpillar in its _____.

  d. Ducks and hens sit on their eggs until they _____.

② English has many words that mean the same thing as each other. We call these words **synonyms**. **Match** the words in column **A** with words in column **B** that mean the same.

A
a. different
b. collect
c. stage
d. beautiful

B
gather
period
lovely
unlike

③ Plural means more than one. **Write the plurals** of these words.

  a. caterpillar: _____   b. stage: _____

④ Most **plurals** end in –s. For words ending in –y, change the –y to –ies to make the plural (e.g., butterfly → butterflies). **Make plurals** out of these words.

  spy _____   fly _____   sky _____

⑤ For most words ending in –f, change –f to –ves in the plural (e.g., leaf → leaves). **Make plurals** out of these words.

  hoof _____   calf _____   elf _____

⑥ Write the **plural** forms of the following words.

  school _____   shelf _____   house _____

  horse _____   baby _____   try _____

LESSON 4: WRITING AN INFORMATION REPORT

🌀 GRAMMAR

Another valuable tool for writers is the **verb**. A verb is a word that does something (action word).

Examples: Peter **talked** to our class.

Meteorologists **study** weather patterns.

A verb can also be a word that tells us something is alive or can be found in a particular place.

Examples: A butterfly **is** a beautiful insect.

A big rock **is** in the middle of the road.

① **Underline** all the **verbs** in these sentences.

  a. Tadpoles grow into frogs.

  b. Ducklings and chickens hatch out of eggs.

  c. The taipan is Australia's most venomous snake.

  d. Monarch butterflies are orange and black and travel in groups of a thousand or more.

  e. Baby turtles hatch from eggs in the sand, then scramble across the beach, dive into the water, and swim out to sea.

Information reports are usually written as if they are happening now. We call this writing in the **present tense**. We know the tense from the verb in the sentence.

Example: Kangaroos **carry** their babies in a pouch.

② Write these sentences in the present tense by changing the verb.

  a. Blue-ringed octopuses lived in tide pools.

  _____

  b. Funnel-web spiders trapped insects in sticky webs around their hole.

  _____

  c. The magpie began life as an egg, hatched into a fledgling, and then grew into an adult bird.

  _____

  _____

③ Look at part of Mele's report below. Underline all the verbs and then circle the sentence that is not in the present tense.

Kangaroos are marsupials. Like all marsupials, they raise their babies in a pouch. The pouch was warm and soft. It is comfortable and safe for the baby joeys.

🌀 PUNCTUATION

When we **list** things (names, actions), we separate them each with a **comma**.

Example: Many animals live only in Australia. Some of these are koalas**,** kangaroos**,** wombats**,** platypuses**,** and echidnas.

LESSON 4: WRITING AN INFORMATION REPORT

✱ PUNCTUATION (cont.)

Insert all the missing commas.

Lions tigers jaguars cheetahs and the common house cat all belong to the same family, the feline family. Wolves coyotes and foxes are all relatives of our pet dogs.

✱ FUN WITH WORDS

① Think about your life. Then on a separate piece of paper **draw** a careful life cycle diagram to illustrate your life through all its stages from past to present. Draw an arrow from one stage to the next and label each stage (e.g., birth → baby → preschool).

② People and animals are alike in lots of ways. In English we have many animal sayings to describe something well known about a person. **Match** the sayings in **A** to the right person in **B**.

A
a. as lazy as a pig in mud
b. as mad as a wet hen
c. as hungry as a horse
d. as sly as a fox
e. as strong as an ox
f. as vain as a peacock

B
thinks he or she is special
is not to be trusted
won't work
is very strong
is extremely angry
hasn't eaten

③ See if you can **make up** some new animal sayings to describe these people.

   a. a very noisy person → as noisy as a _____

   b. a very busy person → as busy as a _____

   c. a very fast runner → as fast as a _____

④ We like to explain things with a **definition** (e.g., An octopus is an eight-armed sea creature.) Here are some funny definitions that can be **completed** with words from the box below. You will not need all of the words.

eraser   net   book   bird   alarm clock   jacket

   a. A _____ is a lot of holes tied up with string.

   b. A _____ _____ will protect a book but will not keep you warm.

   c. An _____ is a small machine for waking people who do not have a rooster.

LESSON 4: WRITING AN INFORMATION REPORT

YOUR TURN TO WRITE

> **TIP FOR TOP WRITERS!**
> When you write an information report:
> - write in the present tense
> - keep your facts in order

Here are some facts about fairy penguins. Using these facts, **write** a report on fairy penguins for your class. Use an encyclopedia to learn more information, if needed. Begin writing your ideas below, then write your final report on a separate sheet of paper.

A fairy penguin . . .
- is a small marine bird
- has very small wings for swimming
- cannot fly
- lives in the waters of southern Australia
- mostly nests on islands
- goes fishing during the day
- returns at night with food for babies
- nests with other fairy penguins in colonies called *rookeries*

Introduction _____
_____
_____

Information (arranged in paragraphs of facts) _____
_____
_____
_____
_____
_____
_____
_____
_____

LESSON 5: Writing a Description of a Person

A **description** of a person is a piece of writing that lets us know that person as well as the writer does.

STRUCTURE | **LANGUAGE**

THE FISHERMAN

Introduction
- man introduced in first sentence
- his work

Mr. Lee was a quiet man. He rarely spoke. A smile and a nod were what we shared. He was mending a net when I first saw him. Squatting on his heels, he was rapidly passing a green net through his fingers. Every so often he stopped to patch a tear or strengthen a weak section that might break under the strain of the good catch he dreamed about.

Verbs all in same tense — this writer uses past tense

Description
- his clothing
- his hands
- his day
- his mood

Every day, an hour before the tide turned, Mr. Lee would appear from among the palm trees that grew down to the beach. He wore a faded blue shirt, ragged shorts, and an old rice-straw hat that almost hid his face. That is probably why I noticed his hands first. For a small, thin man he had big, strong hands. They were hands that could mend a net and cast it, hour after hour, out over the sea.

Carefully-chosen adjectives so reader can "see" his clothes

When his net was ready for the day's work, Mr. Lee would wade out into the sea. Standing knee-deep he would grasp the net evenly between his hands and, in a single graceful movement, cast it out over the water.

Adverbs to show *how* action is done

Sometimes he would hum quietly to himself. Mostly he didn't. He cast his net, pulled it back and cast it again. He was at home in the sea and the sunlight. He was content.

Conclusion
end of his day

When the sun sank low and the sea darkened, he would gather his net and set off back up the beach. Under the trees he prepared his catch of silver fish for sale in the night market. Then he disappeared into the darkness.

Kitty (age 9)

LESSON 5: WRITING A DESCRIPTION OF A PERSON

WHAT DID YOU READ?

① **Circle** the correct answer. Mr. Lee is a . . .

    a. net maker   **b.** fisherman   **c.** beach inspector

② He wears a faded green shirt. **True or false?** _____

③ His hat is made out of _____.

④ **Circle** the correct answer. He fishes from . . .

    a. a boat   **b.** the beach   **c.** shallow water

⑤ Mr. Lee is small and thin. **True or false?** _____

⑥ We know Mr. Lee lives in a warm, tropical place because the trees are _____ trees.

⑦ **a.** Do you think Mr. Lee is a rich man? _____

    b. Why do you think so? _____

_____

HOW IS IT WRITTEN?

① What word in the first sentence tells us that Mr. Lee does not speak very often? _____

② Writers always try to use the most exact words they can. In paragraph 3, what words does this writer use to mean . . .

    a. walk through water? _____   **b.** throw a net? _____

③ Adjectives give detail and interest to descriptions. From paragraph 2, **write** the adjectives that describe Mr. Lee's clothes.

_____

④ A description can tell us about personality by telling us how a person does something. **Circle** the correct answer: *Sometimes he would hum quietly to himself.* This tells us that Mr. Lee is . . .

    a. happy   **b.** bored   **c.** lonely

⑤ Sometimes a writer can tell us something indirectly. *The sun sank low* tells us the time of day is SUN __ __ T.

⑥ In describing the fisherman, the writer refers to his . . .

    a. CL __ __ __ ING   **b.** H __ __ DS

    c. DAY'S W __ __ K   **d.** M __ __ D

⑦ **Circle** the correct answer. A description always keeps the same tense from start to finish. This description is written in the PAST / PRESENT tense.

©Teacher Created Resources, Inc.

LESSON 5: WRITING A DESCRIPTION OF A PERSON

SPELLING AND MEANING

Word Box			
quiet	strengthen	stop	tap
rarely	knee	stopped	tapped
shoulder	knife	gracefully	rapidly

Silent letters are letters that we do not say.

Example: the **k** in **knee**

① **a. Write** one word (not from the word box) under each of these pictures to label it.

 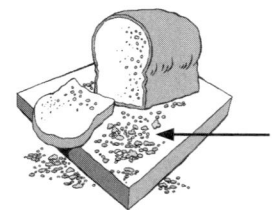 

_____   _____   _____

b. Circle the picture above that does not include a silent letter.

② **Replace** the underlined words below with words from the word box.

    a. We <u>don't very often</u> eat candy. _____

    b. The baby is <u>not making a sound</u>. _____

    c. Muscles <u>get strong</u> with exercise. _____

    d. Ballet dancers move <u>with grace</u>. _____

Vowels (the letters **a**, **e**, **i**, **o**, and **u**) can be pronounced short or long.

Example: t**a**p (short)   t**a**pe (long)

This can change a word's meaning. We know to pronounce the middle vowel long if the word ends in the letter **e**. We call this **bossy e** because it bosses the vowels around.

③ **Circle** the right word.

    a. Kangaroos can hop / hope very fast.

    b. Grapes are grown on the slop / slope of a hill.

    c. Will you mop / mope the floor, please?

④ Using the sto**p** → sto**pped** spelling pattern, **make new words** out of the following:

    mop _____   hop _____   sip _____

    top _____   sop _____   rip _____

    tap _____   sap _____   tip _____

LESSON 5: WRITING A DESCRIPTION OF A PERSON

GRAMMAR

When we write about things that happened in the past, we call this writing in the **past tense**. The verb tells us what tense is being used.

Examples: The postman **stops** at every mailbox. **(present tense)**

The postman **stopped** at every mailbox. **(past tense)**

① **Change** these sentences to past tense by changing the underlined verbs.

a. My dad <u>mops</u> the garage on Saturday. _____

b. Eddie <u>hops</u> on one foot during the game. _____

c. Billy Joe <u>tops</u> the goal chart every season. _____

d. Surveyors <u>map</u> Alaska from the air. _____

② Sam has confused his present and past tenses. Can you help him? **Rewrite** his sentences so that they are all in the **past tense**.

a. The *Titanic* sank when it collides with an iceberg in 1912.

_____

b. Pemulwuy is a brave Aboriginal warrior who lived around Sydney Harbor in the late 1700s.

_____
_____

c. When night falls, bats came out of their cave.

_____

PUNCTUATION—REVISION

① **Insert capitals** and **periods** to separate these sentences.

many people enjoy fishing one of the most dangerous ways to fish is to fish from rocks at the bottom of a cliff big waves often sweep these fishermen into the sea, where many drown

② **Insert** the missing **commas**.

a. Water fleas lobsters crabs and shrimp all belong to the family of crustaceans.

b. Georgie's favorite T-shirt is a holey old red green and blue striped shirt that was given to him when he was six.

c. The Missouri Mississippi Yukon and Rio Grande are the longest rivers in the United States.

d. To own a dog you must feed it train it walk it brush it and love it.

LESSON 5: WRITING A DESCRIPTION OF A PERSON

FUN WITH WORDS

Some words are **counting** words and others are **weighing** words. It is important not to confuse them.

Many and **few** are **counting** words.

Much and **less** are **weighing** words.

Examples: Ali has **many** marbles but Ricky has only a **few**.

Is there **much** more flour than sugar? Yes, but there is **less** salt than flour.

(You can count marbles but you can't count flour, sugar, or salt. You can only pile it up and weigh it.)

More is both a **counting** and a **weighing** word.

Example: Mrs. Jones sells **more** material and buttons than knitting wool and needles.

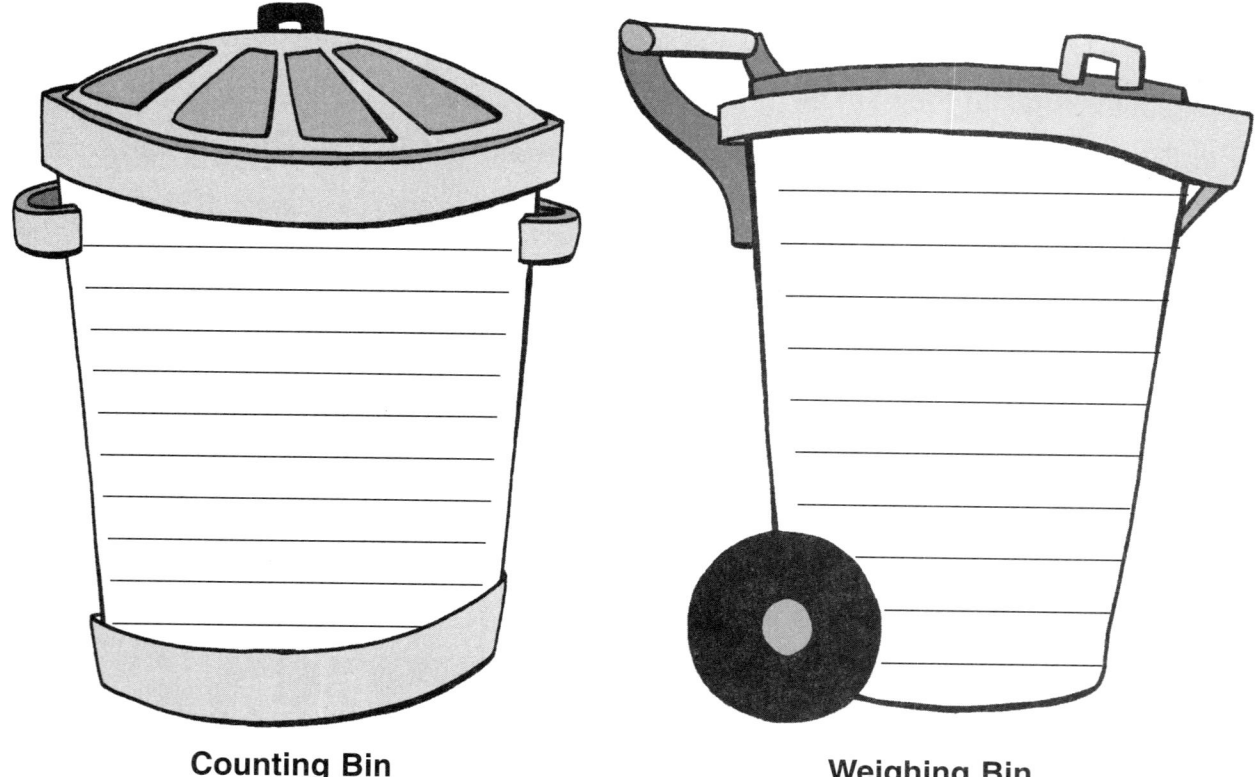

Counting Bin   **Weighing Bin**

① Sort the words from the box below into the right bins above.

cups	rakes	sugar	wheat	cans	letters	powder	ice cream	gates	custard
rice	gravy	jelly	pumpkins	trees	pepper	apples	ice cubes	trucks	soup

② A good way of describing things is to compare them to something else (e.g., The classroom was as busy as a hive of bees.). What do you think these could be **compared to**?

   a. a crowded school bus: _____

   b. lots of people running in different directions: _____

   c. a rainbow in the sky: _____

LESSON 5: WRITING A DESCRIPTION OF A PERSON

JOKE
Q: When were there only three vowels in the alphabet?
A: Before **U** and **I** were born.

YOUR TURN TO WRITE

TIP FOR TOP WRITERS!
Descriptions are word pictures. Pretend you are an artist and paint a picture with words of color, shape, size, and mood.

① The third-grade class at Jefferson Elementary has given us a table of facts about their teacher, Mr. Polly. **Read** them carefully and then **write** a description of Mr. Polly on the lines below.

Is	Has	Does	Can	Wears
tall	long fingers	laughs a lot	be cross	blue shirts
thin	a jolly voice	tells jokes	be very kind	terrible yellow ties
about 40	black hair	plays the piano	sing	gray trousers
strict about homework	olive skin	helps students in trouble	draw dragons	glasses

___
___
___
___
___
___
___
___

② **Think** carefully about your best friend. Think about height and hair color, likes and dislikes, eyes and size, personality and appearance. Think about how you first met, what you liked about your friend at that first meeting, what you play together, and so on.

Then **write** a description of your best friend. Use your own paper for this writing.

LESSON 6 — Writing an Opinion Speech

An **opinion speech** tells the audience what the speaker thinks about something and tries to persuade them to agree with him or her.

STRUCTURE

LANGUAGE

LEARNING TO SWIM

All children must learn how to swim. There are many reasons for this. It's fun and it gives you lots of exercise. The most important reason for learning to swim is that it saves people from drowning.

Firstly, swimming stops many children from drowning. If a child gets caught in a riptide he can swim out of it. If he can't swim, he will most likely drown. Some children drown when they fall into dams and they cannot swim. Other children walk into deep creeks and drown. If they could all swim no one would drown.

Secondly, swimming makes children stronger and healthier. It makes muscles work and get strong. Children get a bit of fresh air in their lungs, too, when they are in the water away from the classroom.

Finally, swimming means you don't just have to play at the edge of the water and on the sand. You can dive straight in and play other sorts of games, like catching waves.

I think it's a very good idea for everyone to learn how to swim. Don't you?

Angela (age 8)

- *Opinion* — all children should learn to swim
- *Argument* — reasons for learning to swim
- *Conclusion* — repeats opinion

- *Example* makes argument believable
- *Numbering* connects arguments and helps audience understand
- *Talks directly* to audience
- *Question* involves audience

LESSON 6: WRITING AN OPINION SPEECH

WHAT DID YOU READ?

① What is the most important reason for learning to swim?
_____

② Give one other reason offered by Angela for learning to swim.
_____

③ **Circle** the right answer. What happens when you are caught in a riptide?
   a. You are swept out to sea.   b. Your bathing suit gets ripped.
   c. You are dumped on the beach.

④ **Circle** the best answer. A dam is . . .
   a. a lake   b. a pond made by people   c. a pool

⑤ **Complete** this sentence. Swimming makes your _____ strong and puts _____ in your lungs.

⑥ What sort of activities do you think you could do in the sand at the water's edge?
_____
_____

⑦ **Circle** the right answer. **Catching a wave** means . . .
   a. filling a bucket with sea water   b. touching a wave
   c. swimming on a wave to the shore

HOW IS IT WRITTEN?

① What is the first sentence of the speech? _____

② What is the second-to-last sentence of the speech? _____
_____

③ These two sentences are almost the same. Why?
   Circle the correct answer.
   a. Angela is reminding her audience of the point of her speech.
   b. Angela has run out of ideas.
   c. Angela likes repeating things.

④ **Circle** the correct answer. The reasons are arranged by number . . .
   a. so the speaker won't forget them   b. to sound intelligent
   c. to help the audience remember the arguments

⑤ **Circle** the right answer. When the speaker says *I think* this suggests that she is . . .
   a. unsure of her facts   b. sincere   c. vain

©Teacher Created Resources, Inc.   37   #8071 Write from the Start! Writing Lessons

LESSON 6: WRITING AN OPINION SPEECH

SPELLING AND MEANING

Word Box	drown	town	edge	dredge
	frown	down	ledge	hedge
	learn	likely	straight	finally

① Can you **write** all the words in the top two lines in alphabetical order? Remember, if the first letters are the same, look at the **second letter** to decide which word comes before the other in the alphabet.

_____   _____   _____   _____

_____   _____   _____   _____

② **Complete** these sentences with words from the word box.

   a. Eagles like to nest on a _____ on the face of a cliff.

   b. A thorny _____ is a safe nesting place for sparrows.

   c. A _____ wrinkled his forehead.

   d. That line is not _____; it is curved.

   e. Those clouds suggest it is _____ to rain today.

③ Can you **make** –*edge* and –*ow* words meaning:

   a. a promise: P __ EDGE   b. a female pig: __ OW

   c. a circus performer: __ __ OW __   d. a drying cloth: __ OW __ L

   e. a light rainfall: __ __ OW __ R   f. a bear's angry voice: G __ OW __

④ **Match** the words in column **A** to their meanings in column **B**.

A
a. likely
b. hedge
c. straight
d. dredge
e. town

B
large village
a river-cleaning barge
probable
a close row of shrubs
without curves

LESSON 6: WRITING AN OPINION SPEECH

GRAMMAR

We know that nouns are words that name things. Two kinds of nouns are common nouns and proper nouns.

Common nouns are general names.

Examples: **country**, **child**, **doctor**

Proper nouns are special names or titles that belong to one thing or one person. Proper nouns always start with a capital letter.

Examples: **India**, **Julie**, **Doctor Habib**

① **Underline** all the proper nouns in this passage.

Cathy Freeman is one of Australia's most famous female athletes. She won medals in three Olympic Games. Cathy lit the torch at the 2000 Olympic Games in Sydney, as well as winning gold in the 400-meter event.

② **Circle** the common nouns and **underline** all the proper nouns in these sentences.

   a. Many famous sportspeople are Aboriginals, including runner Cathy Freeman, AFL player Gavin Wanganeen, and Rugby League player Mal Meninga.

   b. One of our most popular pastimes is swimming. For three months, from June until the end of August, the pools are crowded.

   c. There are twelve months in a year and three months in every season, with March to May being spring and September to November, autumn.

③ The following are all common nouns. Write a **proper noun** related to each one (e.g., river → Ohio River).

Common noun	Proper noun
a. building	
b. country	
c. bridge	
d. man	
e. school	

PUNCTUATION

This passage has lost many of its **capital letters**. Can you **circle** all the letters that should be capitalized?

"waltzing matilda" is australia's most famous song. it was written by andrew barton paterson more than a century ago. at the time, paterson was visiting dagworth station near winton in queensland. "waltzing matilda" was sung in public for the first time on april 6, 1895.

LESSON 6: WRITING AN OPINION SPEECH

FUN WITH WORDS

Words can be used to mean things that, at first glance, seem to have nothing to do with each other.

Examples: Sam's father works in a coal **mine**.

Mr. O'Donnell is a **mine** of information about rivers.

(If you think about it, the connection is that mines contain lots of things people want. People who want to know all about rivers will find all their answers by asking Mr. O'Donnell because he knows so much about rivers.)

① What words in the word box on page 38 would work in these sentence pairs?

   a. My bracelet fell _____ the well.

   I feel very _____ because my brother is sick.

   b. Many fishermen have _____ in the sea.

   I got _____ in that storm.

   c. A margin is a _____ line down the edge of a page.

   He sat _____ down to work without fooling around.

② When we make a speech, we address the people we are talking to by title. Can you **match** these titles and terms of address to their audiences?

Term of address
a. Ladies and Gentlemen
b. Fellow students
c. The Honorable Mr.

Audience
children in your class
judge
group of adults

③ Swimming is an aquatic sport, a sport played in water. The word **aquatic** comes from an old Latin word *aqua*, which means water.

   a. Can you think of three other aquatic sports?

   _____   _____   _____

   b. What is the name of a zoo that only contains fish and other sea creatures?
   A __ __ __ __ __ __ M

④ Puzzle: I live on the sea floor. I am always moving but stay in the same place. I grow but I do not eat anything. I am green and brown and cold and wet. Little fish live in my hair. What am I? I am S __ __ __ __ __ D

LESSON 6: WRITING AN OPINION SPEECH

YOUR TURN TO WRITE

> **TIP FOR TOP WRITERS!**
> A good speech **begins** and **ends** with the **main idea** so that the audience will remember it.

① Imagine you were asked to persuade your school principal to allow your class to visit the zoo. Write, in order of importance, the points you would make to convince the principal.

1. _____
2. _____
3. _____
4. _____
5. _____

② Now outline (below) the speech you would make using the top three points you have written. **Write** your full speech on a separate sheet of paper.

Introduction/Opinion _____

_____

_____

Point 1 _____

_____

_____

Point 2 _____

_____

_____

Point 3 _____

_____

_____

Conclusion _____

_____

_____

LESSON 7

Writing to Persuade: Advertisement

When we write to persuade, we are trying to convince the reader to do something. An **advertisement** is written to **persuade** the reader to **buy** something.

STRUCTURE

- **Title** name of what is being advertised
- **Location** where sale is to be held
- **Details** of goods for sale
- **Necessary information** date, time, and address

LANGUAGE

- **Capital letters** to catch attention for important words
- **Short phrases** very few complete sentences in this advertisement
- **Exclamation marks** to suggest how amazingly good the sale is!
- **Words** to suggest price is cheap
- **Talks directly** to reader

ANNUAL JUNE SALE
TERRIFIC TOYS

Red-Hot Bargains!
Fantastic Specials!
Every day until sold out!

BMX bikes at never-before low prices!
Remote-control cars cheaper than you could believe!

IMAGINE

baby dolls from only $19.99

board games just $12.99

Be the coolest kid on the block with a **Sandman skateboard** at just $39.95

DON'T MISS IT!

Be first in line when the doors open
Monday, June 16 at 9 A.M.

Terrific Toys
56 Prickle Street
Spikey Plains

LESSON 7: WRITING TO PERSUADE: ADVERTISEMENT

WHAT DID YOU READ?

① How often is this sale held? _____

② When will the sale begin? _____

③ When will it end? _____

④ How much will a board game cost? _____

⑤ All baby dolls will cost $19.99. **True or false?** _____

⑥ **Circle** the correct answer. The business holding the sale is . . .

   a. Terrific Toys

   b. Spikey Plains Toy Shop

   c. Sandman Toys

⑦ **Circle** the correct answer. What does Terrific Toys want you to do when you read this advertisement?

   a. look at toys

   b. buy toys

   c. get up early on Monday

HOW IS IT WRITTEN?

① **Circle** the correct answer. This kind of writing . . .

   a. describes a sale

   b. tells a story about a sale

   c. persuades you to go to a sale

② **Circle** the correct answer.

   There are many QUESTION MARKS / EXCLAMATION MARKS in the punctuation of this advertisement.

③ **Circle** the correct answer. The use of punctuation marks is meant to make you feel . . .

   a. surprise   **b.** excitement   **c.** fear

④ **Circle** the **wrong** answer. The words *bargain* and *special* tell us the goods on sale are . . .

   a. not well made   **b.** inexpensive   **c.** specially priced for sale

⑤ **Complete** these words in the advertisement that tell us the prices are very, very, cheap:

   F _ _ _ _ _ _ _ C and R _ _-H _ _ .

©Teacher Created Resources, Inc.

LESSON 7: WRITING TO PERSUADE: ADVERTISEMENT

SPELLING AND MEANING

Word Box	annual	bargain	fantastic	cheap
	sale	special	remote	terrific
	sail	believe	control	imagine

Be careful with words that end in **–ic / –ick**. Most adjectives that end with this sound have the spelling **–ic** (e.g., **terrific** and **fantastic**) but some use **–ick** (e.g., **sick**). Most nouns are spelled **–ick** but a few end with **–ic** (e.g., **elastic**).

① Can you **spell** these words?

   a. Something used to build a house: B _ _ _ _

   b. A thin rod of wood: ST _ _ _

   c. Very horrible: HO _ _ _ _ _ _

   d. Thin stretchy material: EL _ _ _ _ _

   e. Not well: S _ _ _

② **Insert** a word from the word box in the spaces.

   a. Christmas is an _____ holiday celebrated around the world.

   b. Do you _____ in fairies?

   c. If I close my eyes I can _____ I am flying like a bird.

   d. To change channels on the television I use the _____.

To use **a** (a cat) and **an** (an egg) correctly, look at the word that follows it.

Rule: Use **an** before a vowel (a, e, i, o, u) and use **a** before consonants (all other letters).

③ **Insert** **a** or **an** in each of the spaces.

   a. He ate ___ apple but not ___ banana.

   b. ___ orangutan is ___ red-haired member of the ape family.

   c. That blade does not have ___ edge. It is blunt.

④ **Complete** the following by inserting **a** and **an** where necessary.

   Jack got ___ award for being ___ great speller. His class had ___ ice cream party and ___ cake, too.

LESSON 7: WRITING TO PERSUADE: ADVERTISEMENT

GRAMMAR

In some kinds of writing (e.g., in poetry and advertisements), we often use phrases instead of sentences. A **phrase** is a group of words without a verb.

Examples: Red-Hot Bargains!   Annual June Sale

① **Write S** (sentence) or **P** (phrase) at the end of each of the following.

   a. John wants to sell his skateboard. _____
   b. Unbeatable prices! _____
   c. before the end of March _____
   d. on the top shelf _____
   e. Compare prices before you buy. _____

Adverbs tell us how, when, and where something is done.

Examples: Pham ran **quickly** to the mailbox. (how)

It is best to eat **after** swimming, not **before**. (when)

Cows are grazing over **there** on the hill. (where)

② **Circle** all the adverbs in these sentences.

   a. The book sale will begin tomorrow.
   b. Music played and little flags fluttered overhead at the carnival.
   c. The shoppers trudged wearily homeward.
   d. Advertisements for the bonfire night must be sent today.
   e. Breezes gently shifted the leaves of the old gum tree.

③ Adverbs are often used in phrases. **Underline** the adverb in each of these phrases.

   a. over here
   b. on sale tomorrow
   c. fantastic prices everywhere
   d. bright sunlight overhead
   e. after the party

PUNCTUATION

When we exclaim, we are showing surprise, excitement, or alarm in our voices. To show this in writing we use an **exclamation mark (!)**.

Examples: Ouch! Fantastic! Watch out!

We also use an exclamation mark to show a sudden loud noise.

Examples: Bang! Crash! Thump!

Insert an exclamation mark after the words that show strong feelings like surprise, excitement, or alarm.

   a. Bang The balloon burst and scared us all.
   b. Screech The brakes locked tight and the car skidded.
   c. Help Help was the cry from inside the jammed elevator.
   d. Penny and Nijmeh read the warning. Danger No swimming

LESSON 7: WRITING TO PERSUADE: ADVERTISEMENT

FUN WITH WORDS

Many years ago a candy-maker invented a new candy and gave it a wonderful name to describe what it was, how delicious it was, and how happy it would make people. That name was Lollygobbleblissbomb. The new sweet was a best seller in the candy shops.

① Can you **invent** names for these things—names so special people will want to rush out and buy them?

    a. a sticky, chewy, nutty candy on a stick _____

    b. a tiny one-person car with no doors, only a lift-up lid _____

    c. a fluffy pink toy pig that grunts and trots _____

② **Annual** events happen only once a year. **Write** the names of at least three annual events you know of.

    a. _____

    b. _____

    c. _____

③ **a.** The Olympic Games are an annual event. **True or false?** _____

    b. Ramadan and Easter occur annually. **True or false?** _____

    c. Chinese New Year occurs annually. **True or false?** _____

④ You want to sell the following things. Can you think of good, persuasive words to describe each one in an advertisement? **Write** at least two persuasive words under each picture below.

LESSON 7: WRITING TO PERSUADE: ADVERTISEMENT

YOUR TURN TO WRITE

> **TIP FOR TOP WRITERS!**
> When you write an advertisement:
> - Keep it short.
> - Use exciting words.
> - Include details of time, place, and price.

① One Tree School is going to hold a game night. **Sketch** an advertisement in the box persuading people to come.

Make sure you **include**:
- where it will be held
- when it will begin
- how much it will cost

Write and color your final copy on a separate sheet of blank paper.

② **Imagine** you have been asked to write the advertisement for your favorite snack to persuade people to taste it and buy it. **Sketch** that advertisement in the box.

Write your final copy on a separate sheet of blank paper. Include colors and pictures to make your advertisement look attractive.

LESSON 8: Writing a Procedure

A **procedure** is a piece of writing that tells someone what to do or how to do it.

Alex is a new student at Williga Public School. The principal has asked John to help make Alex welcome. He gave John the following instructions so the two boys can meet and walk to school together.

STRUCTURE | **LANGUAGE**

- **Aim** → *title*
- **Walking instructions** in the order that John should follow them
- **Special instructions**
- **Each instruction** begins with a verb and is written as a command
- **Exact details** including names and measurements
- **Explanation** for previous instruction

WALKING TO SCHOOL WITH ALEX

1. **Walk** down Cave Road to Hill Street.
2. **Turn** left onto Hill Street.
3. **Walk** about **100 feet** along Hill Street then turn right onto Shady Lane.
4. Meet Alex on the corner at the end of **Shady Lane**.
5. Walk down the hill along **Gumnut Drive**.
6. Continue along the river, over the creek at Buckley's Crossing, and up the hill.
7. Turn left onto Boronia Road and then into our school.

Don't forget to walk in single file over Buckley's Crossing. It is narrow and dangerous.

I will expect you at my office at 9 A.M.

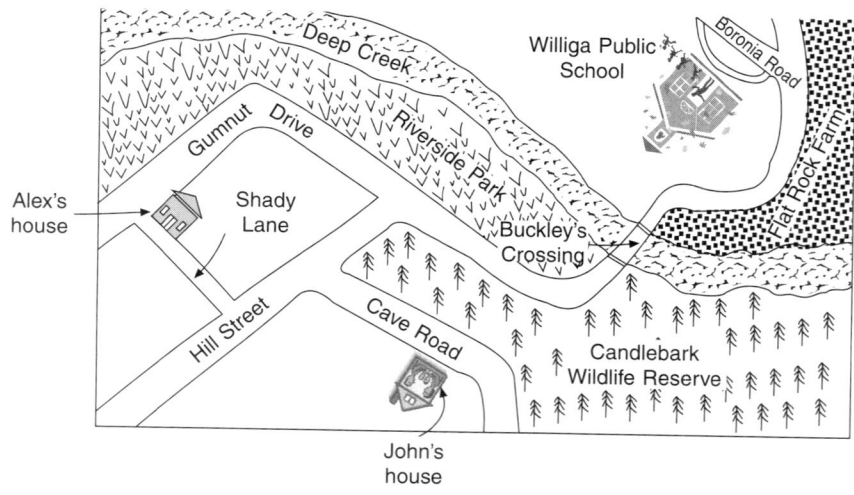

#8071 Write from the Start! Writing Lessons

LESSON 8: WRITING A PROCEDURE

WHAT DID YOU READ?

① **Circle** the correct answer. The principal gave John these instructions so that . . .
   a. he can find Alex's house
   b. he will cross the creek safely
   c. he can walk to school with Alex

② Alex lives on Boronia Road. **True or false?** _____

③ **Circle** the correct answer. Who lives on Hill Street?
   a. Alex   b. John   c. neither

④ When John walks down Cave Road, does he turn right or left onto Hill Street? _____

⑤ Why must the boys walk in single file over Buckley's Crossing?
_____

⑥ Following the instructions, draw the route to school on the map.

HOW IS IT WRITTEN?

① **Circle** the correct answer. What sort of writing is this?
   a. a story
   b. a set of instructions
   c. a description of a town called Candlebark

② **Circle** the correct answer. These instructions are written as . . .
   a. commands   b. questions   c. simple sentences

③ **Circle** the correct answer. The first word in each instruction is . . .
   a. a noun   b. a verb
   c. an adjective   d. an adverb

④ **Circle** the correct answer. The instructions are numbered . . .
   a. to make them clearly understandable
   b. to save time
   c. to look important

⑤ **Circle** the two **wrong** answers. These written instructions include . . .
   a. street directions
   b. a warning
   c. details about Flat Rock farm
   d. house location
   e. an appointment time

LESSON 8: WRITING A PROCEDURE

SPELLING AND MEANING

Word Box	instruction	welcome	race	face
	follow	election	racing	facing
	correction	dangerous	direction	narrow

Spelling rule: For words that end in –*ce*, drop the –*e* when you add –*ing*.

① Following this rule, **add –*ing*** to these words.

  a. pace _____

  b. lace _____

  c. dice _____

  d. ice _____

  e. trace _____

② **Choose** words from the word box to complete the sentences.

  a. Only bikes can go down that lane. It is too _____ for cars.

  b. Deep water is _____ for non-swimmers.

  c. "_____ home," said Lucy's mother on her return.

  d. _____ these instructions carefully.

③ **Match** the words in column **A** to their meanings in column **B**.

A		B
a. correction		north, south, east, west
b. direction		not wide
c. narrow		making right
d. instruction		telling how

④ Words that are **opposite** in meaning are called **antonyms**. **Match** these words with their antonyms.

Word		Antonym
a. dangerous		unwelcome
b. follow		safe
c. narrow		lead
d. welcome		wide

SPELLING AND MEANING (cont.)

⑤

These caterpillars are crawling in S _ _ _ _ _ F _ _ _ _ .

GRAMMAR

Instructions are **always** written in the **present tense**.

Example: **Follow** the gravel road until you **reach** the highway.

Instructions are **always** written as **commands**. Instructions have no subject, only a verb and an object: Verb + Object.

Example: Stop (verb) the noise (object).

① **Rewrite** the following sentences in the present tense as instructions.

a. They rode bikes to school.

b. We never fooled around at the pool.

c. You listened to the instructions carefully.

When we write about things that will happen in the future we use the **future tense** of the verbs in our sentences.

Example: It **will rain** tomorrow.

② These sentences are written in the past tense. **Rewrite** them in the **future tense** by changing the verb.

a. Lucy walked to school.

b. The thunderstorm made walking dangerous.

c. The rules of the game were hard to follow.

③ In what tense are these sentences written? **Write** *past*, *present*, or *future* beside each.

a. Recipes are directions for cooking food. _____

b. Our coach's instructions helped us win the game. _____

c. The stationmaster will tell us when the next train leaves. _____

LESSON 8: WRITING A PROCEDURE

PUNCTUATION—REVISION

Add all missing punctuation, including capitals, commas, and periods in the sentence below.

emily ellie esther and eric all belong to the same family, the edwards family

FUN WITH WORDS

① **Label** each picture with a single word. Use the words from the word box on page 50 to help you.

a. _____ b. _____ c. _____ d. _____

② The box below contains a list of landmarks on the way to Mount Silly Top.

Giggle Pond	Rough Slope
Laughing Rock	Greasy Lane
Jelly Roll Road	Mudbath Hollow
The Sleepy Tree	Joke Corner

a. Draw a picture of one of these landmarks in the empty box.

b. Make up three instructions to get to the landmark you have just drawn. Use some of the other landmark names in your instructions.

1. _____
2. _____
3. _____

c. Stand up. Follow the instructions below carefully. When you get to the end, write down where you are.

1. Take three steps to the right.
2. Turn left and take three more steps.
3. Turn left again and take three more steps.

4. Turn right and take three steps, then turn right and take three more.
5. Turn right and take six steps.
6. Turn right and take three final steps.

Where are you? _____

LESSON 8: WRITING A PROCEDURE

YOUR TURN TO WRITE

> **TIP FOR TOP WRITERS!**
> When you write instructions, remember to make them simple, clear, and chronological (in the right order).

① Mr. Muddle wants to look at the mountains through his binoculars. This is what he does:

   1. He takes the binoculars out of the case.

   2. He adjusts the focus so he can see clearly.

   3. He holds them to his eyes.

   4. He takes the covers off the lenses.

Mr. Muddle can't see the mountains. All he can see is a smudgy blur. Check what Mr. Muddle did, then **write** his **instructions** for adjusting and using his binoculars correctly. Make sure you write the instructions in the correct order. The first is done for you.

1. Take your binoculars out of their case.

2. _____

3. _____

4. _____

② **Write** your friend a set of **instructions** for getting to your house from school.

_____
_____
_____
_____
_____
_____

③ Pretend that you are going on vacation. **Write instructions** for your neighbor to feed your pet while you are away. If you don't have a pet, instruct your neighbor to do something else for you while you are away. Use a separate sheet of paper.

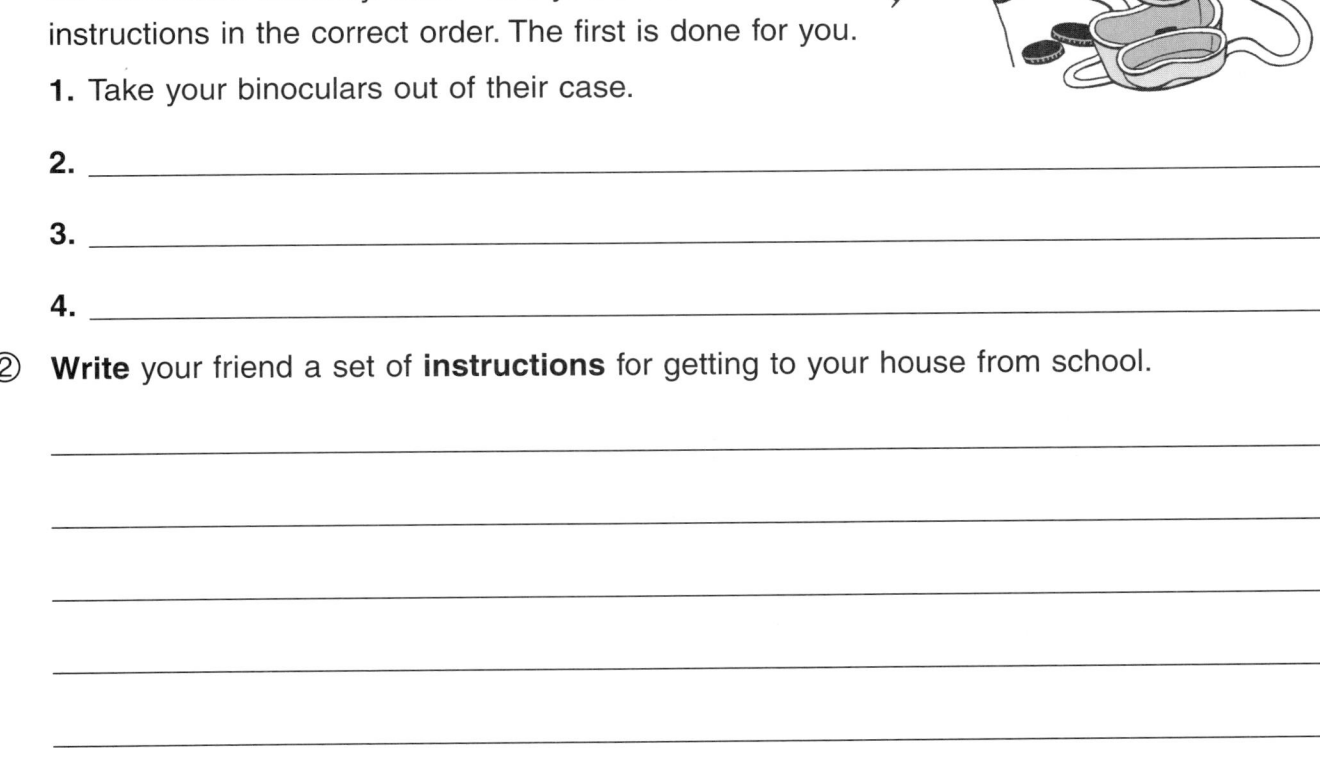

LESSON 9: Writing an Invitation and a Thank-You Letter

An **invitation** is written in a mixture of short sentences and points. It gives all necessary information and encourages the reader to accept.

A **thank-you letter** is a short letter with an address, a date, a greeting, and a signature. It says thank you at its beginning and its end.

STRUCTURE | **LANGUAGE**

- Greeting
- Invitation
- Necessary information
- Personal message
- Signature

- Complete sentences
- Phrases in point form
- Means "please respond"

BIRTHDAY PARTY INVITATION

Dear Sally,
I'll be nine on Saturday.
Please come and help me celebrate at my house.

Where: 14 Marlowe Crescent, Biloxi
When: 2–5 P.M. Saturday, October 9
RSVP: October 6
Phone: 475-0326

I hope you can come.
Your friend,
Peter

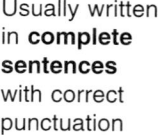

LETTER OF THANKS

14 Marlowe Crescent
Biloxi
October 15, 2005

Dear Grandpa and Grandma,

Thank you for the book about ships. It is a great birthday present. My friend Shane likes ships too, so we are reading it together.

My birthday party was fun. It didn't rain, even though the weather man said it would. We played games and ate lots of ice cream and birthday cake.

Mom made the cake. It was shaped like a ship with licorice for funnels and candy for portholes. It looked very real. It was almost a pity to eat it, but we did.

Dad says he will drive us all up to see you. Emma and I hope it will be very soon. Thank you again for my book.

Love from,

Peter

- Writer's address and the date
- Greeting
- Introduction and thank you
- Body of letter details of party
- Conclusion repeats thanks
- Signature
- Everything starts at left margin

- Usually written in **complete sentences** with correct punctuation

LESSON 9: WRITING AN INVITATION AND A THANK-YOU LETTER

WHAT DID YOU READ?

1. **Complete** this sentence.

   _____ is inviting _____ to his birthday party.

2. Where exactly will the party be held? _____

3. How old will Peter be on Saturday? _____

4. **Complete** this sentence.

   The party will be held between the hours of _____ and _____ o'clock on Saturday.

5. Who is Peter's friend? _____

6. Of what were the portholes made? _____

7. Who made Peter's cake? _____

8. What did Peter's grandparents give him for his birthday?

   _____

9. **Complete** this sentence. Peter wrote this letter to say _____ to his grandparents.

HOW IS IT WRITTEN?

1. **Circle** the **wrong** answer.
   Peter's invitation contains . . .

   a. short sentences

   b. points

   c. dates

   d. explanation of party games

2. **Underline** the **three** most important things in an invitation.

   a. date and time

   b. pictures of balloons and streamers

   c. venue (place)

   d. name of host (birthday person)

   e. special message from host

3. The reason for writing Peter's letter is clear in the first line. **True or false?** _____

4. Peter's thank-you letter talks only about the book he received. **True or false?** _____

5. A letter always starts with a G _ _ _ _ _ _ G and ends with a
   S _ _ _ _ _ _ _ E.

LESSON 9: WRITING AN INVITATION AND A THANK-YOU LETTER

SPELLING AND MEANING

Word Box				
	invitation	real	licorice	Saturday
	weather	reel	ferry	present
	whether	birthday	fairy	celebration

When you are learning to spell, sometimes it helps to break up the words into parts (**syllables**).

Examples: invitation: in / vi / ta / tion   Saturday: Sat / ur / day

① **Write** the words from the word box that have only one syllable.
_____

② Break the following words into syllables. Use a slash (/) to separate them.
   a. present _____
   b. birthday _____
   c. celebration _____
   d. licorice _____

③ The word box contains some **homophones** (words that sound the same but are spelled differently and mean different things). **Choose** the correct word that is a homophone for these pictures.

   a. _____   **b.** _____   **c.** _____

④ **Insert** a word from the word box in the spaces.
   a. You can cross Boston Harbor by _____.
   b. Stormy _____ is dangerous for sea travel.
   c. Eating _____ can stain your tongue black.
   d. Elephants are _____, but dragons are not.

⑤ *Celebrate* is a verb. *Celebration* is a noun. Following the *celebrate/celebration* pattern, make nouns out of these verbs.
   a. decorate _____   **b.** excavate _____
   c. imitate _____   **d.** renovate _____

#8071 Write from the Start! Writing Lessons   56   ©Teacher Created Resources, Inc.

LESSON 9: WRITING AN INVITATION AND A THANK-YOU LETTER

GRAMMAR

Sometimes we write short sentences with only one verb. We call these **simple sentences**.

Example: Balloons are fun.

We can join two simple sentences with a **comma** and the word **and** or **but** to make a longer sentence called a **compound sentence**.

Example: Balloons are fun. Balloons break easily. (two simple sentences)

Balloons are fun**,** *but* balloons break easily. (compound sentence)

① **Join** these simple sentences with a **comma** and the word **and** or **but** to make compound sentences.

a. Peter invited Ahmad to his party. Ahmad was not able to come.

b. Your birthday is in summer. My birthday is in winter.

c. A mouse lives for a year. Some turtles can live for one hundred years.

In a compound sentence we can use another word (a **pronoun**) instead of repeating the **noun**.

Example: Balloons are fun, but **they** break very easily.

They is a **pronoun**. Other pronouns are *I*, *we*, *you*, *he*, *she*, and *it*.

② Join these sentences to make compound sentences using **and** or **but** and a **pronoun**. The first has been done for you.

a. John went to the store. John bought twenty red balloons.

   John went to the store, and he bought twenty red balloons.

b. Katherine cut the cake. Katherine passed a slice to everyone.

c. Billy liked the birthday cake. Billy liked the toffee apples better.

LESSON 9: WRITING AN INVITATION AND A THANK-YOU LETTER

PUNCTUATION

Addresses always start with capital letters, and **months** and **days** of the year do, also.

① Look at the address on Peter's letter and then put **capitals** in the correct places on these addresses.

   a. 4 boulder drive, rocky point
   b. 312 blackberry road, thorny hills
   c. 13 lonely lane, lost horizon
   d. 9 rose place, flowerpot

② **Punctuate** these dates correctly.

   a. october 24, united nations day
   b. march 17, st patricks day

FUN WITH WORDS

① The fun part of a party is the games we play. Can you play the game of authors? In this game you have to listen to the sound of the words and then match the authors' names to the names of their books (e.g., *Cliff Death* by Eileen Dover). Can you hear the meaning in the author's name? **Match** these book titles with their authors' names.

   a. *George in Jail*   by _____   Mary Christmas
   b. *Sleepless Nights*   by _____   Teresa Green
   c. *On a Desert Island*   by _____   Eliza Wake
   d. *Colors in Nature*   by _____   E. Dunnit
   e. *My Favorite Holiday*   by _____   Bob Down
   f. *Knocked Out*   by _____   I. Malone

② How many **one-syllable words** can you make out of the word **celebration**?

   _____   _____   _____
   _____   _____   _____
   _____   _____   _____

③ It is a custom in many countries to associate a precious stone with the month of your birthday (e.g., a person whose birthday is in April has a diamond as his or her birthstone).

The following are the names of precious stones. Can you **complete** them?

   a. PE __ RL
   b. R __ BY
   c. EM __ R __ LD
   d. S __ PPH __ RE

#8071 *Write from the Start! Writing Lessons*
©Teacher Created Resources, Inc.

LESSON 9: WRITING AN INVITATION AND A THANK-YOU LETTER

🌀 FUN WITH WORDS (cont.)

④ If you **answer** these party questions correctly and then put the first letter of each answer together, you will have the answer to the mystery word in question 5.

   a. What do you do with a birthday present? You __ __ __ N it.

   b. Girls' presents are usually wrapped in __ __ __ TTY paper.

   c. We send invitations to __ __ K our friends to our party.

   d. There are lots of cakes and __ __ LLIPOPS at a party.

⑤ **Mystery word:** Precious stone only found in Australia: __ __ __ __

🌀 YOUR TURN TO WRITE

> TIP FOR TOP WRITERS!
> - When you write an invitation you must include who, when, and where.
> - When you write a thank-you letter, be sure to say why you are thankful.

① **Write** and decorate an invitation to your best friend, inviting him or her to come to your birthday party. Use your own paper.

② **Write** a short letter to your uncle thanking him for taking you fishing. You could have been fishing from a boat, from a river bank, or from a pier. Outline your letter below, then write your final copy on another sheet of paper.

Address _____

_____

_____

Greeting _____

Thank you _____

_____

What you enjoyed _____

_____

_____

_____

_____

_____

Thank you again _____

Signature _____

LESSON 10: Writing a Response to a Picture

When we write a **response** to a picture, we are writing **facts** (what we see in the picture) and **opinion** (what we think about what is happening in the picture).

STRUCTURE

Introduction — main idea of picture

Facts and opinion

Reaction — what the writer thinks is most important about the picture

WHEN I LOOK AT THIS PICTURE

I see a traffic jam at an intersection. A car has stopped to let a mother dog cross the road in front of it. Three spotted pups are following her.

The driver waits patiently while the dogs trot across the road. Behind his car other cars begin to back up. Soon lots of cars have stopped.

An old lady coming home from shopping puts her vegetables on the sidewalk while she watches the pups anxiously. A little boy is also watching from the sidewalk. He seems very worried about the last little pup.

One of the pups, the smallest, is lagging way behind the others. I think his little legs can't run as fast as the others. He looks like the runt of the litter.

The man in the first car must be a kind man. Even though the traffic is backed up right around the corner he is not moving. He is not even honking his horn. He is just sitting there waiting for all the dogs to cross the road with a smile on his face.

Jack (age 8)

LANGUAGE

Same tense throughout; this writer uses the present tense

Adverbs tell *how* the waiting and the watching is done

Good choice of noun tells us that this is the smallest and weakest of the pups

LESSON 10: WRITING A RESPONSE TO A PICTURE

WHAT DID YOU READ?

① **Complete** this sentence. The traffic is backed up right around _____.

② Why did the first driver stop? _____
_____

③ The pups are all the same size. **True or false?** _____

④ How many pedestrians are watching? _____

⑤ What was the old lady doing before she stopped to watch the dogs?
_____

⑥ **Circle** the statement that is correct.

   a. The smallest pup's legs can't run as fast as his brothers' legs.

   b. Jack thinks the smallest pup's legs cannot run as fast as his brothers' legs.

⑦ Why does the writer think the first driver is kind?
_____
_____

⑧ Who is Jack? _____

HOW IS IT WRITTEN?

① **Circle** the correct answer. The main idea of the picture is explained in paragraph . . .

   a. one   **b.** two   **c.** three

   d. four   **e.** five

② **Complete** the sentence. Jack uses the word P __ __ __ __ __ __ LY to tell us that the driver waited without getting angry.

③ **Circle** the correct answer. Jack tells us . . .

   a. only what he sees

   b. only what he thinks

   c. what he sees and what he thinks about what he sees

④ Response writing includes **facts** (what the writer sees) and **opinion** (what the writer thinks about what he sees). **Complete** these sentences.

   One **fact** in Jack's writing is _____

   One **opinion** in Jack's writing is _____

LESSON 10: WRITING A RESPONSE TO A PICTURE

SPELLING AND MEANING

Word Box

intersection	sidewalk	patient	building
stopped	vegetables	impatient	runt
traffic	anxiously	worried	lagging

Remember to break big words into syllables as you learn to spell them. Take extra care with double letters, as in **worried**. Divide the syllables between double letters (e.g., wor/ried). Use the Look, Cover, Write, and Check way to learn spelling (see page 8).

① **Insert** a word from the word box to complete the sentences.

　a. An _____ man kept pushing the crosswalk button.

　b. The sea captain watched the stormy sky _____.

　c. There are traffic lights at the _____ of Todd and Hope Streets.

　d. Beans, cabbage, and broccoli are all green _____.

② **Match** the words in column **A** to their synonyms in column **B**.

A
a. kind
b. concerned
c. small
d. sidewalk
e. pedestrian

B
walker
little
pavement
anxious
thoughtful

③ The word **bank** has many meanings. Read each sentence carefully and then choose, from the explanations below, the one that best suits the meaning of **bank** in that sentence.

　a. Old Charlie Green fishes from the river **bank**. ___

　b. Mary went to the **bank** to deposit her birthday check. ___

　c. I want to **bank** my pocket money. ___

Explanations

　A **Verb** meaning to save

　B **Noun** meaning a place of business where people have money accounts

　C **Noun** meaning the side of a river

LESSON 10: WRITING A RESPONSE TO A PICTURE

GRAMMAR

When we **compare** one noun to another, we change the form of the adjectives we use.

Example: Mark is **tall**.
Matthew is **taller**.
Luke is **tallest**.

MARK　　　MATTHEW　　　LUKE

① **Write** the correct form of the adjective in parentheses on the line.

  a. Mt. Everest is (high) _____ than Mt. Vesuvius.

  b. The cheetah is the (fast) _____ animal on Earth.

  c. Crimson is the (dark) _____ tone of the color red.

  d. Shrubs are (short) _____ than trees.

For adjectives that end in *–y*, change the **y** to *i* before adding *–er* or *–est*.

  Example: dry → drier → driest

② **Change** these adjectives according to this pattern.

  a. lovely _____ _____
  b. ugly _____ _____
  c. empty _____ _____
  d. friendly _____ _____
  e. hungry _____ _____

Some adjectives have their own special ways of comparing nouns.

  Examples: good → better → best
  far → farther → farthest
  bad → worse → worst

③ **Write** the correct form of the word in parentheses on the line.

  a. John is good at bowling, but Songkai is the (good) _____ bowler.

  b. Our moon is far away, but Jupiter is (far) _____ away.

  c. Neptune is the planet at the end of our solar system. It is (far) _____ from Earth.

  d. All my family members had the flu, but I had it the (bad) _____.

LESSON 10: WRITING A RESPONSE TO A PICTURE

🌀 PUNCTUATION

Insert all the missing punctuation and capital letters in this passage.

there are eight planets in our solar system they are called earth venus mercury mars jupiter saturn uranus and neptune pluto is a dwarf planet at the end of our solar system isn't the solar system amazing

🌀 FUN WITH WORDS

① Many words mean **big**, but some are bigger than others. **Write** these **big** words in the triangle, with the smallest meaning of **big** at the top and the largest at the bottom.

big gigantic huge enormous

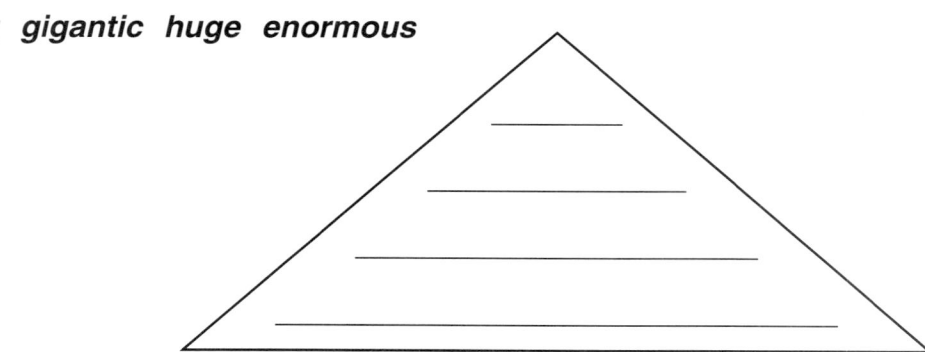

② These are all **little** words. Can you arrange them in order of "littleness," ending with the smallest?

small infinitesimal minute tiny

a. _____ b. _____ c. _____ d. _____

③ Can you **guess** the missing word?

   a. People have _____, pigs have snouts, and elephants have trunks.

   b. Horses have hooves, people have feet, and seals have _____.

   c. Fish have scales, bears have _____, and people have skin.

   d. People live in houses, foxes live in dens, and bees live in _____.

④ Most creatures like to live in groups. Here are some group names. Can you **match** them with the creatures to which they refer?   flock   herd   pride   pod   school   pack

   a. a _____ of fish   b. a _____ of lions

   c. a _____ of wolves   d. a _____ of whales

   e. a _____ of cattle   f. a _____ of birds

⑤ When we gather things together, we often give them group names, too. Can you **complete** these group names?

   a. a group of ships: F __ __ __ T

   b. knives, forks, and spoons together: C __ TL __ __ Y

   c. a group of planes: SQU __ D __ __ N

LESSON 10: WRITING A RESPONSE TO A PICTURE

JOKE
Q: How do you know which end of a worm is its head?
A: Tickle it in the middle and wait till it smiles.

YOUR TURN TO WRITE

TIP FOR TOP WRITERS!
When looking at a picture, ask . . .
- What do I see?
- What do I think?

Look carefully at the pictures above. Choose **one** of these pictures to which to **write** a response, according to the plan below. Use a separate sheet of paper.

Paragraph 1: What is the most important thing happening in the picture?

Paragraph 2: Write some details about the picture.

Paragraph 3: Write some more details about the picture.

Paragraph 4: What do you think when you look at this picture? Would you like to be doing this? How would you feel?

LESSON 11: Writing for School Research Projects

When we are asked to gather information on a subject and present it in a book or on a poster, we can present the information in two ways:

- as an **information report** written in **complete sentences.**
- as a **list of facts** in point form written in **phrases**

STRUCTURE — **LANGUAGE**

INFORMATION REPORT

Koalas

The koala is a small, tree-living marsupial found only in Australia. It used to be called a "native bear." The koala's thick, woolly fur is gray, except on its belly, where it is yellowish-white. It has large, round, furry ears, small, brown eyes, and a big, flat, black nose. Because it lives in trees, it has short powerful arms and legs with strong black nails for climbing.

Koalas usually have only one baby at a time and care for it in a pouch under the mother's belly. When the baby is big, it hangs onto its mother's belly fur with its claws to be carried when she moves around.

- **Physical description** includes definition in first sentence
- **Facts** about life and habitat
- **Several related facts** in one sentence
- **Adjectives** of shape, size, color, and texture
- **All verbs** in present tense throughout text

FACT BOXES

Habits	Dangers
• usually solitary	• timber cutting
• mostly nocturnal	• feral animals
• rarely drinks	• disease called *chlamydia*
• eats only eucalyptus leaves	• spread of houses
• clumsy on ground	• speeding traffic

- **Titles** tell us what kind of facts are in the boxes
- **Bullets,** numbers, letters, etc. highlight facts
- **All facts** presented as short phrases

SAMPLE LAYOUTS

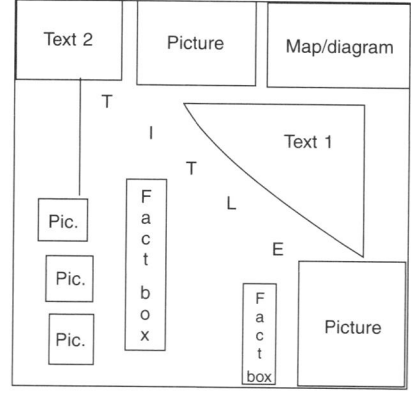
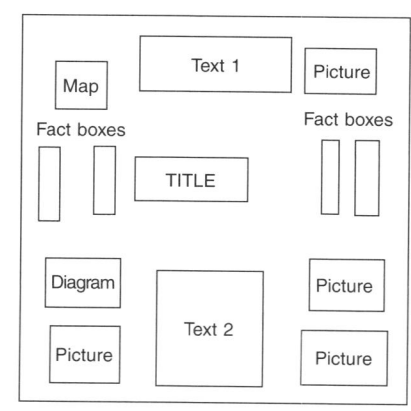

LESSON 11: WRITING FOR SCHOOL RESEARCH PROJECTS

WHAT DID YOU LEARN?

Complete these sentences about the **information report**.

① The information report is written in S __ NT __ __ CES.

② This text D __ SCR __ B __ S what a _____ looks like and why it looks like that.

③ It includes details such as color and size so we can S __ __ a picture of a koala in our minds.

④ It does N __ T include any opinions, only F __ __ TS.

Complete these sentences about the **fact boxes**.

① These are written in P __ __ NT form.

② Points are N __ T complete sentences. They are PH __ __ S __ S.

③ Each point tells us a F __ __ T about the koala or its environment.

④ Points could be listed by N __ __ B __ R, by L __ TT __ R, by symbols like stars, or by bullet points.

⑤ The facts in each fact box are all related. Facts in Box 1 are all about the K __ __ L __ and those in Box 2 are all about D __ NG __ RS to koalas.

Complete these sentences about the **sample layouts**.

① There is only one way to arrange a layout. **True or false?** _____

② Look at both layouts. The following usually occur in all layouts. Can you complete these words?

a. T __ TL __

b. I __ F __ __ M __ TION R __ P __ __ TS

c. P __ CT __ __ __ S

d. F __ __ T BOXES

YOUR TURN TO WRITE

① **Read** the passage and then **write** the most important facts about the blue whale in point form in the **fact box** below.

Our ocean waters are home to so many different kinds of whales. Some of the most interesting are the baleen whales, which do not have teeth. Instead, they have fringes of whalebone, or baleen, hanging in fine strips from the roofs of their mouths. They swim with their mouths open, and the baleen strains tiny sea creatures called *krill* out of the water as their huge tongues push the water out through the baleen.

The largest of all the whales is the blue whale. The blue whale belongs to the baleen whale family. It can eat 3 tons of food—the weight of 6 cars—in one day! It is the largest mammal that has ever lived, measuring, on average, 80 feet and weighing up to 130 tons.

Blue whale

FACT BOX

- _____
- _____
- _____
- _____
- _____
- _____

LESSON 11: WRITING FOR SCHOOL RESEARCH PROJECTS

YOUR TURN TO WRITE (cont.)

② Do some research and **write** a **fact box** about one of the following: bats   brush fires   policemen   stars   dolphins   seals   parrots   farms   volcanoes   earthquakes

Title: _____

- _____
- _____
- _____
- _____
- _____
- _____

③ **Read** the facts in the fact box below. Then **rewrite** them as an **information report**. Don't forget to write in complete sentences. Outline your report below, then write your final information report on a separate sheet of paper. Do your own research to find more interesting facts.

The sperm whale
- 60 feet long
- huge square head
- largest toothed whale
- several rows of teeth
- once killed for its oil
- now protected

ANSWER KEY

LESSON 1   PAGES 6–11

What did you read?
① Kevin's dad
② on the farm where Kevin lived
③ in Bungendore
④ False
⑤ False
⑥ a, c
⑦ was not
⑧ to hold the house securely on the trucks

How is it written?
① True
② c
③ interesting
④ anything that interested you
(e.g., moving the house in two halves)
⑤ b
⑥ a

Spelling and meaning
① a. halves
   b. elves
   c. calf
   d. shelves
② a. calf
   b. halves
   c. shelves
   d. elf
③ a. half
   b. shelves
   c. elves
   d. calves
   e. halves

Grammar
① a. (Neil Armstrong) walked ⟨on the moon.⟩
   b. (Snakes) eat ⟨small birds.⟩
   c. (Storm clouds) fill ⟨the sky.⟩
   d. (Mr. Patel) drives ⟨a moving truck.⟩
② a. no
   b. yes
   c. yes
   d. no
③ Possible answers:
   a. Five children played marbles.
   b. All our class plays soccer.
   c. Mrs. Mercado packed her good china.
   d. A moving truck moved our furniture.
   e. The garden tools are in that shed.

ANSWER KEY

Punctuation
① a. period
   b. question mark
   c. period
② In the countryside there are no traffic jams to worry drivers. **I**nstead, drivers have to worry about dust. **W**hy is this so**? B**ig trucks leave great clouds of dust in the air, and this makes it hard for drivers behind them to see where they are going.

Fun with words
① a. cow
   b. shelves
   c. elves
   d. half
② kangaroo, joey
③ a. furniture
   b. boxes
   c. truck
   d. pack
   e. removal
   f. wrap

Your turn to write
① e, b, c, d, a, f OR e, b, d, c, a, f

LESSON 2 — PAGES 12-17

What did you read?
① a bottle with a message inside
② c
③ The dolphin swallowed them.
④ a starfish
⑤ The dolphin took them there.
⑥ 15 years
⑦ a. Yes, Triton fed them, but not very well.
   b. They ate only seaweed and plankton.
⑧ c

How is it written?
① b
② a
③ trailed
④ Landcrabs, does not
⑤ "King Triton wants to see you." **or** "The king is about to make an announcement." **or** "You will build me a house for every creature in my world, even the smallest of them."

Spelling and meaning
② a. very tiny sea creatures
   b. sharp, snapping sound
   c. any living animal or person
   d. bodies of saltwater covering ¾ of Earth
③ a. tough, enough
   b. fruit, bruise

Grammar
① cupboard, Monday, horse, America, field, church, shop, ship, illness, George
② a. Charlie, beach, sun, sand, surf
   b. flags, beach
   c. seashells, homes, mollusks
   d. starfish, points, arms
   e. tide, moon
③ wave, dolphin, ball, fin, beak, eyes, tail, flippers, ocean, water

Punctuation
When winter is over, everyone is happy. **P**eople wear sandals and sun hats. **C**hildren go swimming. **A**dults begin to garden again. **S**mall plants grow tall and seeds turn into plants. **E**ven birds are happy and busy building nests.

ANSWER KEY

Fun with words

① a. octopus
   b. shark's, seal's
   c. calf
   d. seahorse
   e. swordfish
   f. starfish
② a. box
   b. engine
   c. angry
   d. cub
   e. hollow
   f. beach
③ a. coral
   b. blue whale
④

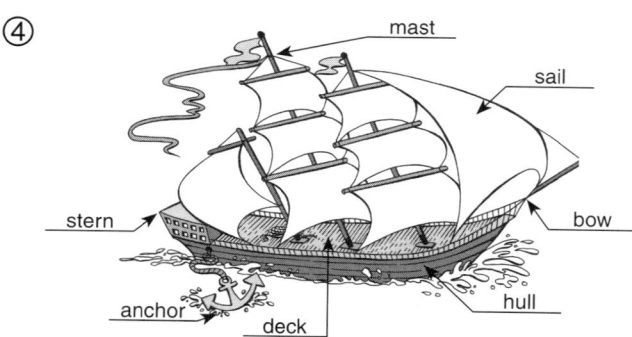

LESSON 3   PAGES 18–23

What did you read?

① c
② False
③ We know it is not afraid of people because it sits on Eric's shoulder.
④ b
⑤ round
⑥ False
⑦ no
⑧ a

How is it written?

① Brat rat,/pet rat,/my rat/in my hand.
② black and white/beady eyes bright
③ shells
④ pink snake tail
⑤ a
⑥ a, b, e

Spelling and meaning

① a. beach
   b. sight
   c. paint
   d. light
   e. dainty
② a. paint
   b. beach
   c. saint
③ a. teach
   b. reach
   c. leash
④ a. sight, light, tight
   b. same

Grammar

① a. sleek, smooth, brown, black
   b. long, bare, strong, tiny, useless
   c. old, shabby, crooked
   d. sweet-smelling, comfortable, pet
   e. empty, sad, lost
② a. new, clumsy
   b. happy, tropical, glass
   c. same, lonely
   d. rough, bad-tempered
   e. green, gentle
③ a. leafy
   b. sandy
   c. dirty
   d. angry
   e. hungry
   f. friendly

ANSWER KEY

Punctuation

① a. Seal pups are fat**,** round**,** roly-poly balls of soft fur.
   b. Magpies build big**,** strong nests high up off the ground.
   c. Crimson rosellas flash scarlet**,** blue**,** and green in flight.
   d. Keeping pets is an interesting**,** enjoyable**,** and responsible hobby.

Fun with words

① <u>Scales</u>: snake, goldfish, python
   <u>Fur</u>: rat, mouse, guinea pig, wombat, dog, cat, bear
   <u>Feathers</u>: eagle, magpie, penguin, canary, parrot
   <u>Skin</u>: frog, lizard, whale
② a. sty
   b. stable
   c. burrow
   d. den
   e. coop
③ a. zoologist
   b. apiarist
   c. stockman
   d. veterinarian
④ a. fur
   b. feathers
   c. burrow
   d. bill
   e. ocean
   f. hooves

LESSON 4 — PAGES 24–29

What did you read?

① b
② a caterpillar
③ leaves
④ It builds a chrysalis.
⑤ a
⑥ dry
⑦ to collect pollen

How is it written?

① Butterflies are born caterpillars. All caterpillars become butterflies.
② a. hatch
   b. pollen
③ b
④ c

Spelling and meaning

① a. pollen
   b. leaves
   c. chrysalis
   d. hatch
② a. unlike
   b. gather
   c. period
   d. lovely
③ a. caterpillars
   b. stages
④ spies, flies, skies
⑤ hooves, calves, elves
⑥ schools, shelves, houses, horses, babies, tries

Grammar

① a. grow
   b. hatch
   c. is
   d. are, travel
   e. hatch, scramble, dive, swim
② a. Blue-ringed octopuses live in tide pools.
   b. Funnel-web spiders trap insects in sticky webs around their hole.
   c. The magpie begins life as an egg, hatches into a fledgling, and then grows into an adult bird.
③ are, raise, was, is. The pouch was warm and soft.

ANSWER KEY

Punctuation

Lions, tigers, jaguars, cheetahs, and the common house cat all belong to the same family, the feline family. Wolves, coyotes, and foxes are all relatives of our pet dogs.

Fun with words

② a. won't work
   b. is extremely angry
   c. hasn't eaten
   d. is not to be trusted
   e. is very strong
   f. thinks he or she is special
④ a. net
   b. book jacket
   c. alarm clock

LESSON 5   PAGES 30-35

What did you read?

① b
② False
③ rice straw
④ c
⑤ True
⑥ palm
⑦ a. Mr. Lee is not a rich man.
   b. His clothes and work tell us he is poor.

How is it written?

① quiet
② a. wade
   b. cast
③ faded blue, ragged, old rice-straw
④ a
⑤ sunset
⑥ a. clothing
   b. hands
   c. day's work
   d. mood
⑦ past

Spelling and meaning

① a. cat, crumbs, lamb
   b. cat
② a. rarely
   b. quiet
   c. strengthen
   d. gracefully
③ a. hop
   b. slope
   c. mop
④ mopped, hopped, sipped, topped, sopped, ripped, tapped, sapped, tipped

Grammar

① a. mopped
   b. hopped
   c. topped
   d. mapped
② a. The *Titanic* sank when it **collided** with an iceberg in 1912.
   b. Pemulwuy **was** a brave Aboriginal warrior who lived around Sydney Harbor in the late 1700s.
   c. When night **fell**, bats came out of their cave.

Punctuation–Revision

① **M**any people enjoy fishing. **O**ne of the most dangerous ways to fish is to fish from rocks at the bottom of a cliff. **B**ig waves often sweep these fishermen into the sea, where many drown.
② a. Water fleas, lobsters, crabs, and
   b. holey, old, red, green, and
   c. Missouri, Mississippi, Yukon, and
   d. feed it, train it, walk it, brush it, and

Fun with words

① **Counting**: cups, rakes, cans, letters, ice cubes, pumpkins, trees, apples, gates, trucks
Weighing: sugar, wheat, powder, ice cream, custard, rice, gravy, jelly, pepper, soup

ANSWER KEY

LESSON 6 — PAGES 36-41

What did you read?
① The most important reason for learning to swim is to prevent people from drowning.
② It strengthens muscles. **or** It puts fresh air in the lungs. **or** You don't just have to play at the edge of the water.
③ a
④ b
⑤ muscles, fresh air
⑥ build sand castles, collect shells, dig pools and rivers
⑦ c

How is it written?
① All children must learn how to swim.
② I think it's a very good idea for everyone to learn how to swim.
③ a
④ c
⑤ b

Spelling and meaning
① down, dredge, drown, edge, frown, hedge, ledge, town
② a. ledge
   b. hedge
   c. frown
   d. straight
   e. likely
③ a. pledge
   b. sow
   c. clown
   d. towel
   e. shower
   f. growl
④ a. probable
   b. a close row of shrubs
   c. without curves
   d. a river-cleaning barge
   e. large village

Grammar
① Cathy Freeman, Australia's, Olympic Games, Cathy, Olympic Games, Sydney
② a. **Common**: sportspeople, runner, player, player
   Proper: Aboriginals, Cathy Freeman, AFL, Gavin Wanganeen, Rugby League, Mal Meninga
   b. **Common**: pastimes, swimming, months, pools
   Proper: June, August
   c. **Common**: months, year, months, season, spring, autumn
   Proper: March, May, September, November

Punctuation
"**W**altzing **M**atilda" is **A**ustralia's most famous song. **I**t was written by **A**ndrew **B**arton **P**aterson more than a century ago. **A**t the time, **P**aterson was visiting **D**agworth **S**tation near **W**inton in **Q**ueensland. "**W**altzing **M**atilda" was sung in public for the first time on **A**pril 6, 1895.

Fun with words
① a. down
   b. drown
   c. straight
② a. group of adults
   b. children in your class
   c. judge
③ a. synchronized swimming, diving, water polo, water skiing, etc.
   b. aquarium
④ seaweed

LESSON 7 — PAGES 42-47

What did you read?
① It is held once a year.
② It will begin on Monday, June 16.
③ The sale will end when all of the goods are sold.
④ $12.99

⑤ False
⑥ a
⑦ b

How is it written?
① c
② exclamation marks
③ b
④ a
⑤ fantastic, red-hot

Spelling and meaning
① a. brick
   b. stick
   c. horrific
   d. elastic
   e. sick
② a. annual
   b. believe
   c. imagine
   d. remote
③ a. an apple, a banana
   b. An orangutan, a red-haired member
   c. an edge
④ Jack got **an** award for being **a** great speller. His class had **an** ice cream party and **a** cake, too.

Grammar
① a. S
   b. P
   c. P
   d. P
   e. S
② a. tomorrow
   b. overhead
   c. wearily
   d. today
   e. gently
③ a. here
   b. tomorrow
   c. everywhere
   d. overhead
   e. after

Punctuation
a. Bang!
b. Screech!
c. Help! Help!
d. Danger! No swimming!

Fun with words
③ a. False
   b. True
   c. True

LESSON 8   PAGES 48–53

What did you read?
① c
② False
③ c
④ He turns left.
⑤ They must cross in single file because it is narrow and dangerous.

How is it written?
① b
② a
③ b
④ a
⑤ c, d

ANSWER KEY

Spelling and meaning
① a. pacing
   b. lacing
   c. dicing
   d. icing
   e. tracing
② a. narrow
   b. dangerous
   c. Welcome
   d. Follow
③ a. making right
   b. north, south, east, west
   c. not wide
   d. telling how
④ a. safe
   b. lead
   c. wide
   d. unwelcome
⑤ single file

Grammar
① a. **Ride** bikes to school.
   b. Never **fool around** at the pool.
   c. **Listen** to the instructions carefully.
② a. Lucy **will walk** to school.
   b. The thunderstorm **will make** walking dangerous.
   c. The rules of the game **will be** hard to follow.
③ a. present
   b. past
   c. future

Punctuation–Revision
Emily**, E**llie**, E**sther**,** and **E**ric all belong to the same family**,** the **E**dwards family**.**

Fun with words
① a. follow
   b. narrow
   c. correction
   d. dangerous
② c. You should be standing exactly where you started.

LESSON 9   PAGES 54-59

What did you read?
① **Peter** is inviting **Sally** to his birthday party.
② at Peter's house on 14 Marlowe Crescent, Biloxi
③ nine years old
④ The party will be held between the hours of **two** and **five** o'clock.
⑤ Shane
⑥ candy
⑦ his mother
⑧ a book about ships
⑨ thank you

How is it written?
① d
② a, c, d
③ True
④ False
⑤ greeting, signature

Spelling and meaning
① reel, real
② a. pre / sent
   b. birth / day
   c. ce / le / bra / tion
   d. lic / or / ice
③ a. ferry
   b. real
   c. whether
④ a. ferry
   b. weather
   c. licorice
   d. real

ANSWER KEY

⑤ a. decoration
b. excavation
c. imitation
d. renovation

Grammar

① a. Peter invited Ahmad to his party, but Ahmad was not able to come.
b. Your birthday is in summer, and my birthday is in winter.
c. A mouse lives for a year, but some turtles can live for one hundred years.

② a. John went to the store, and he bought twenty red balloons.
b. Katherine cut the cake, and she passed a slice to everyone.
c. Billy liked the birthday cake, but he liked the toffee apples better.

Punctuation

① a. 4 **B**oulder **D**rive
Rocky **P**oint
b. 312 **B**lackberry **R**oad
Thorny **H**ills
c. 13 **L**onely **L**ane
Lost **H**orizon
d. 9 **R**ose **P**lace
Flowerpot

② a. **O**ctober 24, **U**nited **N**ations **D**ay
b. **M**arch 17, **St**. **P**atrick's **D**ay

Fun with words

① a. E. Dunnit
b. Eliza Wake
c. I. Malone
d. Teresa Green
e. Mary Christmas
f. Bob Down

② ate, bale, bar, beat, beer, belt, bit, bite, bone, born, brat, car, cone, core, eat, in, lane, late, lean, lee, leer, lent, lit, nail, near, neat, note, on, rail, rant, rat, rate, real, rear, reel, rent, rib, role, rote, rub, tail, tale, tar, tea, tear, tone (and you may be able to find some more)

③ a. pearl
b. ruby
c. emerald
d. sapphire

④ a. open
b. pretty
c. ask
d. lollipops

⑤ opal

LESSON 10   PAGES 60–65

What did you read?

① the corner
② The first driver stopped to allow the mother dog and her pups to cross the road.
③ False
④ Two
⑤ She was shopping for vegetables.
⑥ b
⑦ The first driver is kind because he stopped, and he is not honking his horn.
⑧ Jack wrote the response to the picture.

How is it written?

① a
② patiently
③ c
④ a. Possible facts include: traffic jam, dog has three pups, lady and boy are watching dogs
b. The driver of the first car is a kind man.

ANSWER KEY

Spelling and meaning

① a. impatient
  b. anxiously
  c. intersection
  d. vegetables
② a. thoughtful
  b. anxious
  c. little
  d. pavement
  e. walker
③ a. C
  b. B
  c. A

Grammar

① a. higher
  b. fastest
  c. darkest
  d. shorter
② a. lovelier, loveliest
  b. uglier, ugliest
  c. emptier, emptiest
  d. friendlier, friendliest
  e. hungrier, hungriest
③ a. better
  b. farther
  c. farthest
  d. worst

Punctuation

There are eight planets in our solar system. They are called Earth, Venus, Mercury, Mars, Jupiter, Saturn, Uranus, and Neptune. Pluto is a dwarf planet at the end of our solar system. Isn't the solar system amazing?

Fun with words

① Answers may vary.

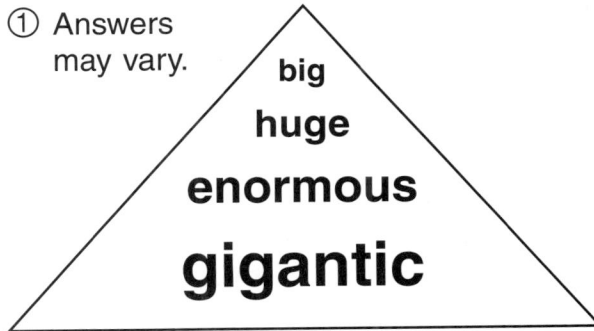

② a. small
  b. tiny
  c. minute
  d. infinitesimal
③ a. noses
  b. flippers
  c. fur
  d. hives
④ a. school
  b. pride
  c. pack
  d. pod
  e. herd
  f. flock
⑤ a. fleet
  b. cutlery
  c. squadron

LESSON 11 PAGES 66-69

What did you learn?

Information report:
① sentences
② describes, koala
③ see
④ not, facts

ANSWER KEY

Fact boxes:
① point
② not, phrases
③ fact
④ number, letter
⑤ koala, dangers

Sample layouts:
① False
② a. title
   b. information reports
   c. pictures
   d. fact boxes

Your turn to write

①
- largest mammal on Earth
- belongs to toothless-whale family; called *baleen whales*
- has baleen instead of teeth
- baleen used to sieve food from water
- main food, krill
- average size 80 feet, 130 tons
- eats 3 tons of food in one day